Francis Frith's

Around Andover

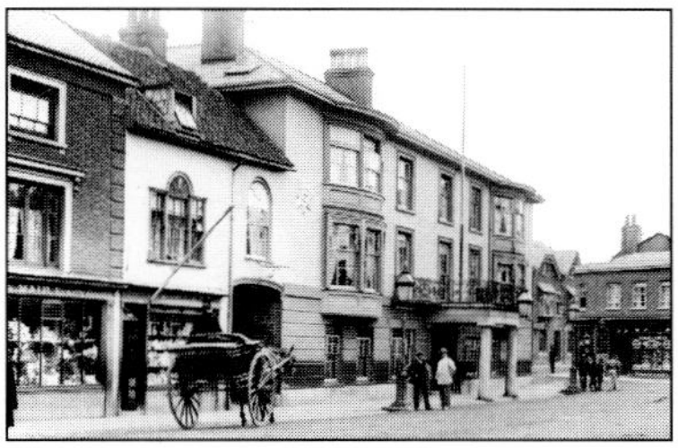

Photographic Memories

Francis Frith's
Around Andover

John MacDonald

FRITH BOOK Co

First published in the United Kingdom in 2001 by
Frith Book Company Ltd

Paperback Edition 2001
ISBN 1-85937-292-9

British Library Cataloguing in Publication Data

Francis Frith's Around Andover
John MacDonald

Frith Book Company Ltd
Frith's Barn, Teffont,
Salisbury, Wiltshire SP3 5QP
Tel: +44 (0) 1722 716 376
Email: info@francisfrith.co.uk
www.francisfrith.co.uk

Printed and bound in Great Britain

Front Cover: Andover, Bridge Street 1913 65317

Acknowledgements
My thanks are due to friends and acquaintances who allowed me time in discussing aspects of this book, answering my questions and adding to, or confirming its content. They included Mrs F Judson, who gave me the recent history of the workhouse site, Miss June Mary Harris, Mrs Pat Simmonds, Mrs Mary Edmunds, Mr H W Earney, and Mr and Mrs John Cox, who shared reminiscences with me, and in particular, Mr Derek J Tempero for his interest, patience and advice in reviewing the final stages of copy. I must also mention Margaret, my wife, who burned the midnight oil in the final stages.

The following publications were among those consulted and found to be invaluable:
Andover, A Pictorial History by Derek J Tempero, 1991, Phillimore & Co Ltd, Chichester.
Andover, An Historical Portrait by John Spaul, 1977, BAS Press Limited.
Old Andover by C J J Berry, Standard Press, 1976. *Inns of Andover* by H W Earney, Holmes & Sons (Printers), 1997.
The Buildings of England: Hampshire and Isle of Wight by Nicholas Pevsner/David Lloyd, 1967, Penguin Books.

AS WITH ANY HISTORICAL DATABASE THE FRITH ARCHIVE IS CONSTANTLY BEING CORRECTED AND IMPROVED
AND THE PUBLISHERS WOULD WELCOME INFORMATION ON OMISSIONS OR INACCURACIES

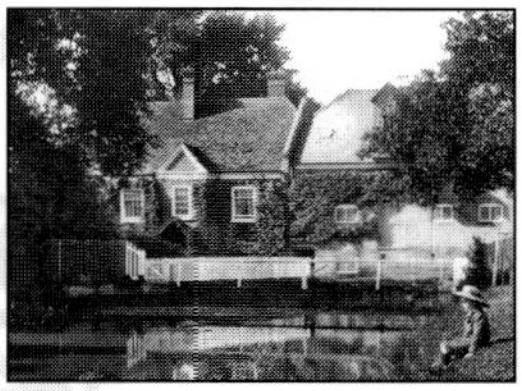

Contents

Francis Frith: *Victorian Pioneer*

Francis Frith, Victorian founder of the world-famous photographic archive, was a complex and multi-talented man. A devout Quaker and a highly successful Victorian businessman, he was both philosophic by nature and pioneering in outlook.

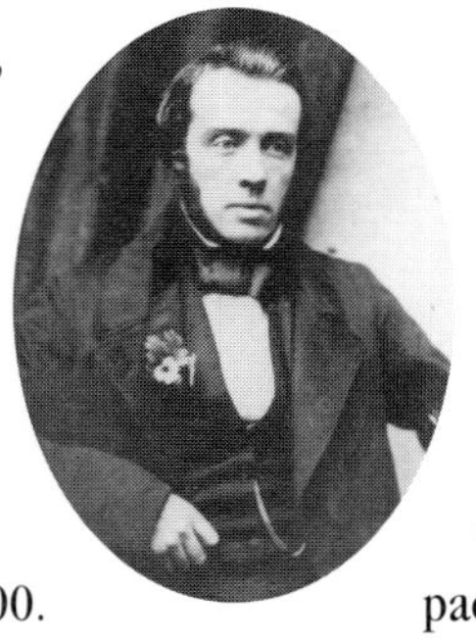

By 1855 Francis Frith had already established a wholesale grocery business in Liverpool, and sold it for the astonishing sum of £200,000, which is the equivalent today of over £15,000,000. Now a multi-millionaire, he was able to indulge his passion for travel. As a child he had pored over travel books written by early explorers, and his fancy and imagination had been stirred by family holidays to the sublime mountain regions of Wales and Scotland. 'What a land of spirit-stirring and enriching scenes and places!' he had written. He was to return to these scenes of grandeur in later years to 'recapture the thousands of vivid and tender memories', but with a different purpose. Now in his thirties, and captivated by the new science of photography, Frith set out on a series of pioneering journeys to the Nile regions that occupied him from 1856 until 1860.

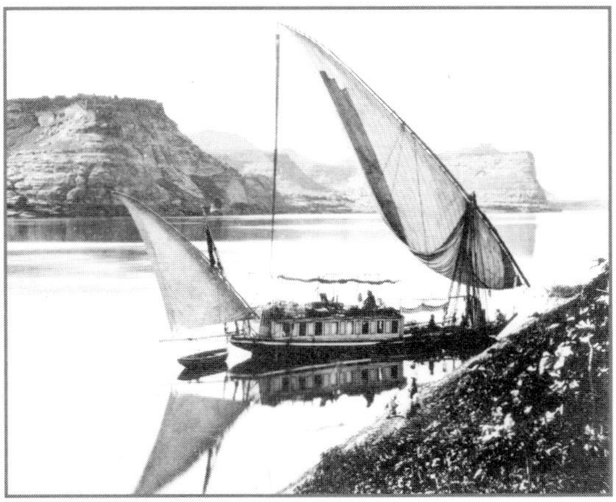

Intrigue and Adventure

He took with him on his travels a specially-designed wicker carriage that acted as both dark-room and sleeping chamber. These far-flung journeys were packed with intrigue and adventure. In his life story, written when he was sixty-three, Frith tells of being held captive by bandits, and of fighting 'an awful midnight battle to the very point of surrender with a deadly pack of hungry, wild dogs'. Sporting flowing Arab costume, Frith arrived at Akaba by camel seventy years before Lawrence, where he encountered 'desert princes and rival sheikhs, blazing with jewel-hilted swords'.

During these extraordinary adventures he was assiduously exploring the desert regions bordering the Nile and patiently recording the antiquities and peoples with his camera. He was the first photographer to venture beyond the sixth cataract. Africa was still the mysterious 'Dark Continent', and Stanley and Livingstone's historic meeting was a decade into the future. The conditions for picture taking confound belief. He laboured for hours in his wicker dark-room in the sweltering heat of the desert, while the volatile chemicals fizzed dangerously in their trays. Often he was forced to work in remote tombs and caves where conditions were cooler. Back in London he exhibited his photographs and was 'rapturously cheered' by members of the Royal Society. His reputation as a photographer was made overnight. An eminent modern historian has likened their impact on the population of the time to that on our own generation of the first photographs taken on the surface of the moon.

Venture of a Life-Time

Characteristically, Frith quickly spotted the opportunity to create a new business as a specialist publisher of photographs. He lived in an era of immense and sometimes violent change. For the poor in the early part of Victoria's reign work was a drudge and the hours long, and people had precious little free time to enjoy themselves. Most had no transport other than a cart or gig at their disposal, and had not travelled far beyond the boundaries of their own town or village. However, by the 1870s, the railways had threaded their way across the country, and Bank Holidays and half-day Saturdays had been made obligatory by Act of Parliament. All of a sudden the ordinary working man and his family were able to enjoy days out and see a little more of the world.

With characteristic business acumen, Francis Frith foresaw that these new tourists would enjoy having souvenirs to commemorate their days out. In 1860 he married Mary Ann Rosling and set out with the intention of photographing every city, town and village in Britain. For the next thirty years he travelled the country by train and by pony and trap, producing fine photographs of seaside resorts and beauty spots that were keenly bought by millions of Victorians. These prints were painstakingly pasted into family albums and pored over during the dark nights of winter, rekindling precious memories of summer excursions.

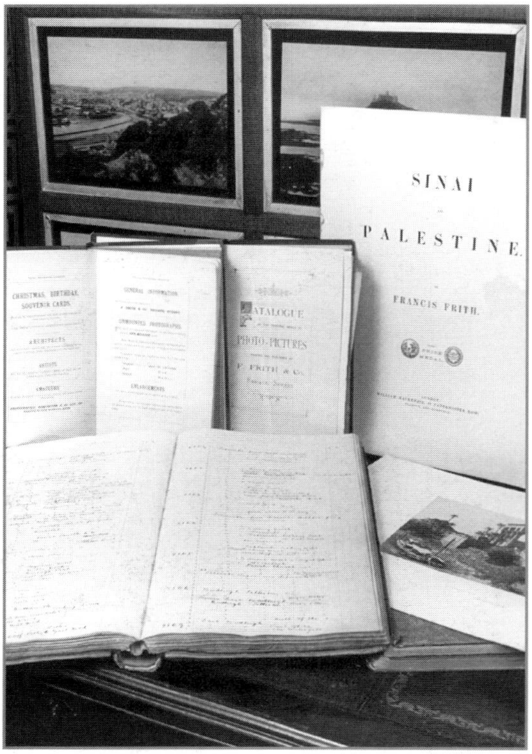

The Rise of Frith & Co

Frith's studio was soon supplying retail shops all over the country. To meet the demand he gathered about him a small team of photographers, and published the work of independent artist-photographers of the calibre of Roger Fenton and Francis Bedford. In order to gain some understanding of the scale of Frith's business one only has to look at the catalogue issued by Frith & Co in 1886: it runs to some 670 pages, listing not only many thousands of views of the British Isles but also many photographs of most European countries, and China, Japan, the USA and Canada – note the sample page shown opposite from the hand-written *Frith & Co* ledgers detailing pictures taken. By 1890 Frith had created the greatest specialist photographic publishing company in the

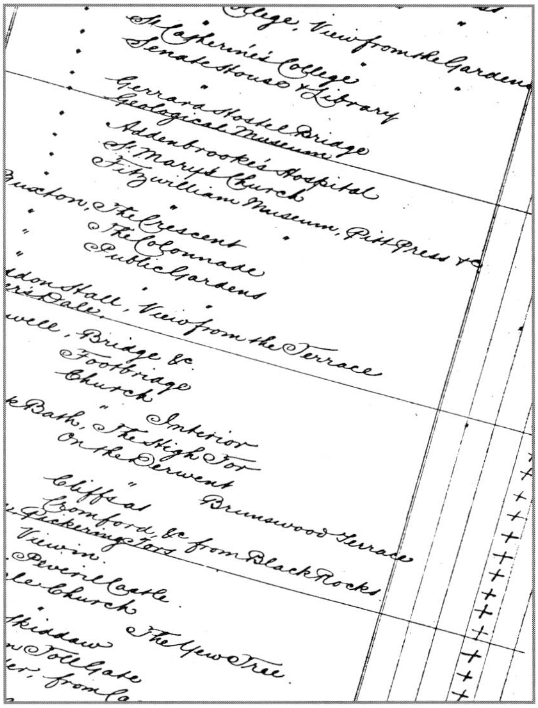
...llege, View from the Garden
St Catherine's College
Senate House & Library
Gerrards Hostel Bridge
Geological Museum
Addenbrooke's Hospital
St Mary's Church
Fitzwilliam Museum, Pitt Press &c
...uxton, The Crescent
" The Colonnade
" Public Gardens
...don Hall, View from the Terrace
...rs Dale.
...well, Bridge &c.
Footbridge
Church
" Interior
...k Bath, The High Tor
On the Derwent
Cliffs at
" Brunswood Terrace
Cromford, &c from Black Rocks
...Pickering Tors
View in
Peveril Castle
...le Church
The Yew Tree
...kiddaw
...n Toll Gate
...er, from Ca...

world, with over 2,000 outlets – more than the combined number that Boots and WH Smith have today! The picture on the right shows the *Frith & Co* display board at Ingleton in the Yorkshire Dales. Beautifully constructed with mahogany frame and gilt inserts, it could display up to a dozen local scenes.

Postcard Bonanza

The ever-popular holiday postcard we know today took many years to develop. In 1870 the Post Office issued the first plain cards, with a pre-printed stamp on one face. In 1894 they allowed other publishers' cards to be sent through the mail with an attached adhesive halfpenny stamp. Demand grew rapidly, and in 1895 a new size of postcard was permitted called the court card, but there was little room for illustration. In 1899, a year after Frith's death, a new card measuring 5.5 x 3.5 inches became the standard format, but it was not until 1902 that the divided back came into being, with address and message on one face and a full-size illustration on the other. *Frith & Co* were in the vanguard of postcard development, and Frith's sons Eustace and Cyril continued their father's monumental task, expanding the number of views offered to the public and recording more and more places in Britain, as the coasts and countryside were opened up to mass travel.

Francis Frith died in 1898 at his villa in Cannes, his great project still growing. The archive he created continued in business for another seventy years. By 1970 it contained over a third of a million pictures of 7,000 cities, towns and villages. The massive photographic record Frith has left to us stands as a living monument to a special and very remarkable man.

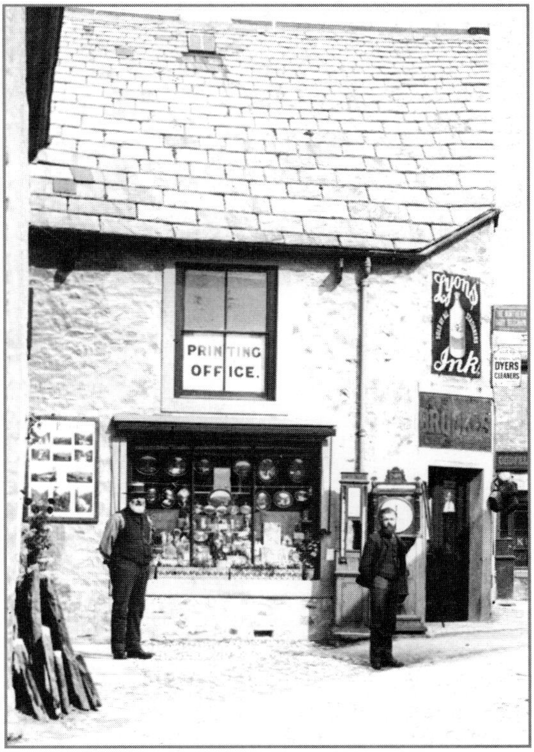

Frith's Archive: *A Unique Legacy*

FRANCIS FRITH'S legacy to us today is of immense significance and value, for the magnificent archive of evocative photographs he created provides a unique record of change in 7,000 cities, towns and villages throughout Britain over a century and more. Frith and his fellow studio photographers revisited locations many times down the years to update their views, compiling for us an enthralling and colourful pageant of British life and character.

We tend to think of Frith's sepia views of Britain as nostalgic, for most of us use them to conjure up memories of places in our own lives with which we have family associations. It often makes us forget that to Francis Frith they were records of daily life as it was actually being lived in the cities, towns and villages of his day. The Victorian age was one of great and often bewildering change for ordinary people, and though the pictures evoke an impression of slower times, life was as busy and hectic as it is today.

We are fortunate that Frith was a photographer of the people, dedicated to recording the minutiae of everyday life. For it is this sheer wealth of visual data, the painstaking chronicle of changes in dress, transport, street layouts, buildings, housing, engineering and landscape that captivates us so much today. His remarkable images offer us a powerful link with the past and with the lives of our ancestors.

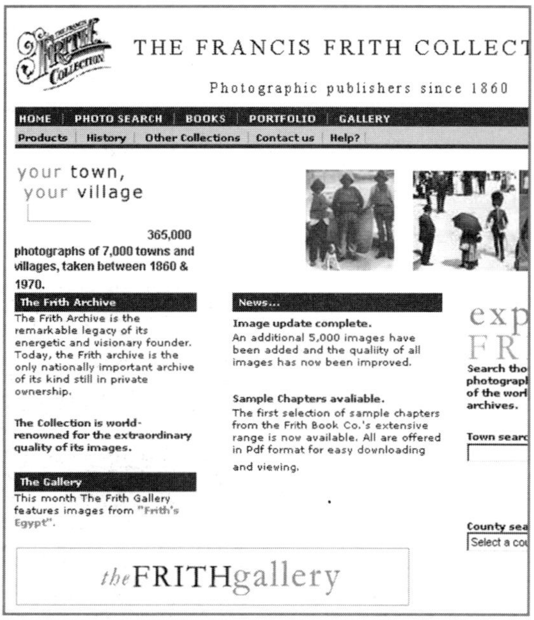

See Frith at www. francisfrith.co.uk

Today's Technology

Computers have now made it possible for Frith's many thousands of images to be accessed almost instantly. In the Frith archive today, each photograph is carefully 'digitised' then stored on a CD Rom. Frith archivists can locate a single photograph amongst thousands within seconds. Views can be catalogued and sorted under a variety of categories of place and content to the immediate benefit of researchers.

Inexpensive reference prints can be created for them at the touch of a mouse button, and a wide range of books and other printed materials assembled and published for a wider, more general readership - in the next twelve months over a hundred Frith local history titles will be published! The day-to-day workings of the archive are very different from how they were in Francis Frith's time: imagine the herculean task of sorting through eleven tons of glass negatives as Frith had to do to locate a particular sequence of pictures! Yet the archive still prides itself on maintaining the same high standards of excellence laid down by Francis Frith, including the painstaking cataloguing and indexing of every view.

It is curious to reflect on how the internet now allows researchers in America and elsewhere greater instant access to the archive than Frith himself ever enjoyed. Many thousands of individual views can be called up on screen within seconds on one of the Frith internet sites, enabling people living continents away to revisit the streets of their ancestral home town, or view places in Britain where they have enjoyed holidays. Many overseas researchers welcome the chance to view special theme selections, such as transport, sports, costume and ancient monuments.

We are certain that Francis Frith would have heartily approved of these modern developments in imaging techniques, for he himself was always working at the very limits of Victorian photographic technology.

The Value of the Archive Today

Because of the benefits brought by the computer, Frith's images are increasingly studied by social historians, by researchers into genealogy and ancestory, by architects, town planners, and by teachers and schoolchildren involved in local history projects.

In addition, the archive offers every one of us an opportunity to examine the places where we and our families have lived and worked down the years. Highly successful in Frith's own era, the archive is now, a century and more on, entering a new phase of popularity.

The Past in Tune with the Future

Historians consider the Francis Frith Collection to be of prime national importance. It is the only archive of its kind remaining in private ownership and has been valued at a million pounds. However, this figure is now rapidly increasing as digital technology enables more and more people around the world to enjoy its benefits.

Francis Frith's archive is now housed in an historic timber barn in the beautiful village of Teffont in Wiltshire. Its founder would not recognize the archive office as it is today. In place of the many thousands of dusty boxes containing glass plate negatives and an all-pervading odour of photographic chemicals, there are now ranks of computer screens. He would be amazed to watch his images travelling round the world at unimaginable speeds through network and internet lines.

The archive's future is both bright and exciting. Francis Frith, with his unshakeable belief in making photographs available to the greatest number of people, would undoubtedly approve of what is being done today with his lifetime's work. His photographs, depicting our shared past, are now bringing pleasure and enlightenment to millions around the world a century and more after his death.

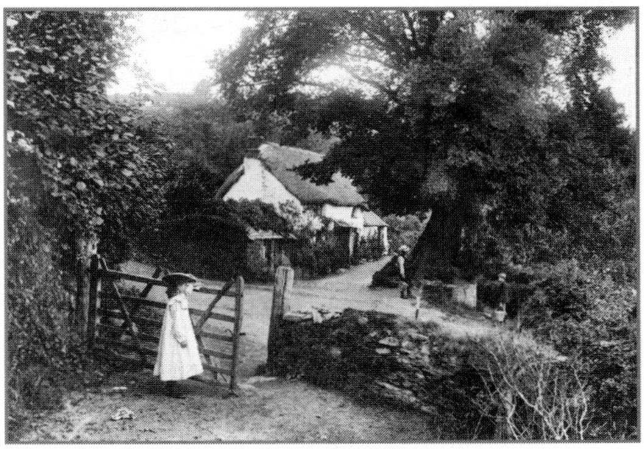

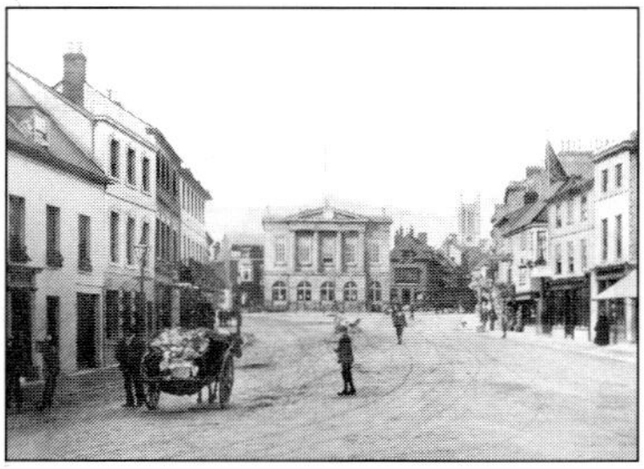

Andover - *An Introduction*

THE MODERN HAMPSHIRE town of Andover, with a population exceeding 41,000, straddles the River Anton in the north-west corner of the valley of the River Test, around 65 miles west of London. It can be reached with relative ease by road or rail from every direction.

For over 4,000 years this has been the site of the crossing of two ancient routes: from London to the West, and the Solent to the Midlands. Irish gold passed through this point to be traded in Europe in the Bronze age. Conquering Romans settled and farmed. Pilgrims passed on their way to Canterbury. Cavaliers and Roundheads swept back and forth in contention. Nearby Weyhill, 'The Greatest Fair in the Kingdom', had half a million sheep on offer in 1700. For over two hundred years, until the mid-19th century, the town bustled with coaches, despite the ruffians of the road.

In 1855 the railway reached the outskirts of the town, beyond Junction Road. Ten years later the 'Sprat and Winkle' branch was built from Andover Junction to Andover Town and on to Redbridge in the outskirts of Southampton. In 1964 Lord Beeching closed this line; today's traveller by train arrives once again at Andover's original station, which for a period was called Andover Junction. In

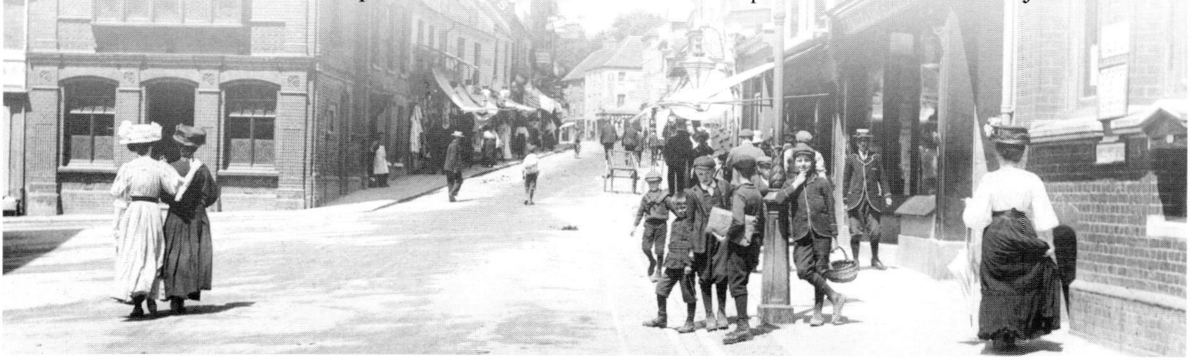

1855, he might have travelled on from this station by pony and trap in the direction of St Mary's Parish Church, the town's most prominent landmark at the top of Church Hill (now Marlborough Street). Today he is more likely to take a bus or a taxi to town.

St Mary's Parish Church, built 1842-6, stands on the site of the Saxon-Norman Church of St Peter. Its presence points to the existence of Andover as a settlement, close to the church and nearby hunting lodge of Saxon Kings, overlooking the river as it weaved its way through the Medieval marshland. It was here that Olaf Trygvasson, leader of a band of marauding Vikings, was persuaded by the Wessex King, Ethelred the Unready, to be confirmed as a Christian in 994 AD. Returning to Trondheim, he became King of Norway and converted his country to Christianity.

By 1086, Andover had six mills and at least 107 inhabitants, with 62 of these described in the Domesday Book as 'villagers'. Today, the Town Mill and Rooksbury Mill remain as rebuilt in Georgian times, but milling ceased after World War Two. They now serve respectively as a busy public house and a fisherman's club. Almost nothing of Cricklade Mill remains but the mill race. Anton Mill only lives on in Frith's picture, and even the names and locations of the other two mills are long forgotten.

The well-drained chalk lands have long enabled sheep and wheat to be successfully farmed around Andover. Wool was the chief source of Andover's prosperity in the Middle Ages and is remembered in place names such as Rack Close. Chalk has another virtue in that it acts as a self-levelling reservoir. Heavy falls of rain seldom result in flooding, as concentrations of deeper water can pass sideways into surrounding chalk, with little effect in a general rise. Consequently, chalk was a stable base for buildings and, on the right site, a basement could be relied upon to be relatively dry.

The scourge of the Middle Ages was leprosy and the response was isolation of the infected. By 1313 Andover had a leper house in the self-supporting hospital of St Mary Magdalene, about a mile along the road to Weyhill.

The Black Death came to Andover in 1603 with catastrophic effect, for the course of the disease was more rapid than leprosy. Families were decimated. The village of Foxcotte virtually disappeared. It took about 50 years and the establishment of nine separate 'pest-houses' outside the town for the plague to die down. The population in 1600 neared 2,000. With almost 1,000 deaths from the plague, it is likely that Andover had only around 1,100 inhabitants by the year 1700.

However, the town survived by virtue of increased travel by coach from about 1650, which brought an expansion in trade. The town grew and prospered, yet the Enclosures Act, like other acts during the 18th and halfway into the 19th century, progressively deprived common farmers and labourers of many of their age-old privileges.

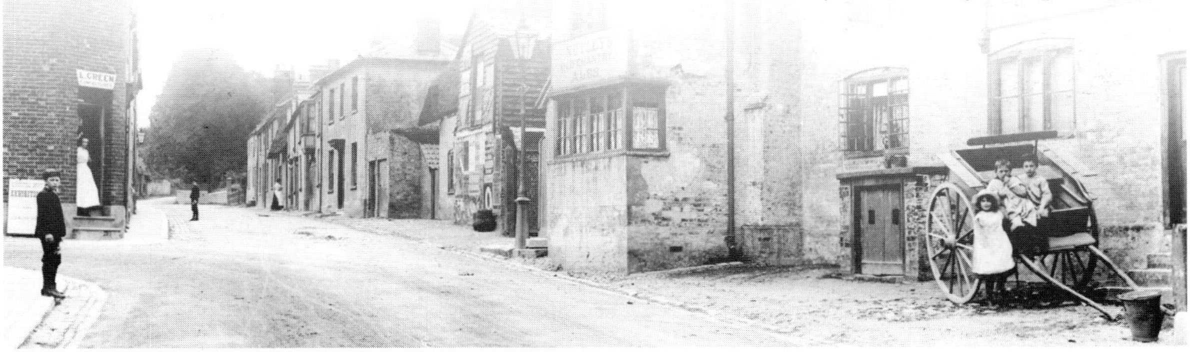

Depression of wages, unemployment, hardship and a drift from the land were the inevitable results. The Andover Enclosure Acts were passed in 1740 and 1784. Meanwhile, the growing industrial revolution increasingly attracted labour into the towns, and by the end of the 18th century, Andover had swelled to about 3,000.

A Hampshire map of 1817 shows the town loosely contained within New Street, the Common Acre (now part of the Recreation Ground), Love Lane, Old Winton Road bottom leg, along the townward side of the River Anton as far as the Folly Inn, and back by Shepherds Spring Lane to New Street.

Grievance against the Corn Laws fuelled riots in 1830 throughout the country. In Andover the mood spread and the Riot Act had to be read. Machines were smashed. Disorder was promptly quelled and arrests made, leading to convictions and transportations.

In spite of this, Andover's population continued to grow to 5,000 by the mid-19th century, until by 1901 it was about 6,500. However, Victorian/Edwardian confidence in the omnipotent power of industry eventually waned, and by the mid-20th century, the Depression and two World Wars had closed Weyhill's 'Greatest Fair in the Kingdom' and slowed the town's growth. It came to be seen as something of a backwater with a population in 1950 of little more than 14,500.

In 1961 Andover Borough Council, Hampshire County Council and the Greater London Council signed an agreement for London overspill to come to Andover, where population would be expected to rise by 31,000 to 48,000 over a 20-year period. This implied an annual growth rate exceeding 1,500, whereas for the 60-year period from 1900, growth had been less than 100 per annum. The agreement was brought to an end before term in 1978, but Andover had already become the fastest growing town in Hampshire. The population may come close to 43,000 in 2002.

Such rapid growth has produced such change that it is a wonder there is anything left of the old town to improve or protect - so much has been swept away or overlaid. Yet the extent of this pain will be offset by the increase in opportunity that the changes have stimulated and which Andover is well-placed to grasp.

A new civic pride has emerged, and in recent years Test Valley Borough Council has made great efforts to improve the town's image. The Upper High Street was repaved in the late 1970s and restricted to pedestrians. There is an annual profusion of planted flowers and hanging baskets. Companies are encouraged to support such displays. Parks have been created both in the centre and out of town, with sculptures and carvings set out in public spaces. Both the town and the villages take part in the annual Test Valley in Bloom competition,

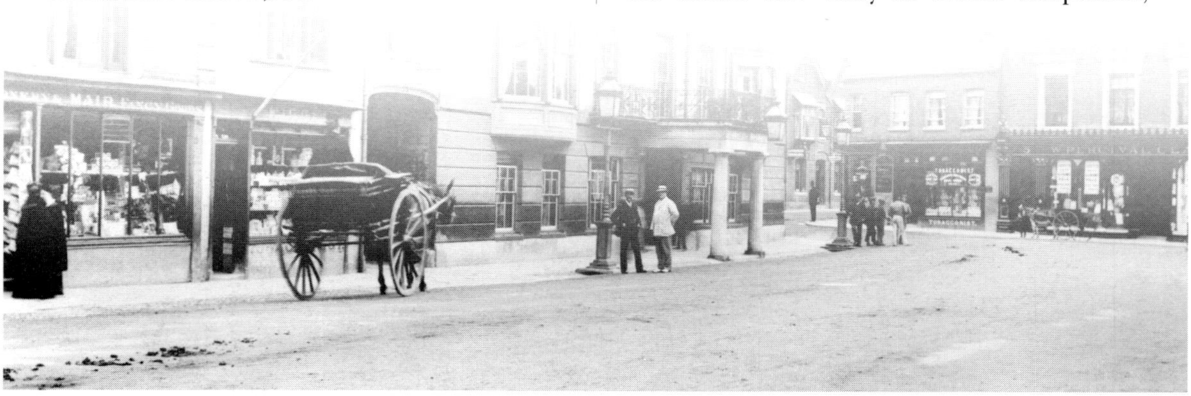

striving to set the highest standard of display.

The west source of the River Anton still rises near Biddesden House and passes the Folly Inn (now the Hungry Horse). It continues towards town with, on the left, the Lloyds TSB Training Centre and Shepherds Spring Lane, now busy with new houses being built. The east feeder momentarily pauses against a weir and then flows through the remains of Cricklade millrace to join the river where the Medieval marshes once were.

On a tree-lined clearing in the crook between the two flows, the stone sculpture of a Red Indian stands and recalls those who in 1643 left for the New World, founding a new Andover in Massachusetts three years later. The figure marks the formal twinning of the two towns in 1999.

The river flows on and, just as it is about to reach the Town Mill, passes a small park with recent sculptures, including the wood-carved fisherman with his flat hat and his catch on his knee, seated on the bench facing the Town Millpond.

Water still rushes through the Town Mill. At the end of the island, brown trout can often be seen in the quiet, willow-shaded waters, where the rushing flow meets calm water. It is possible that fish such as these have been seen here for many centuries. On a wave-topped stone on the island are carved two lines from Tennyson's poem 'The Brook': 'I chatter chatter as I flow to joint the brimming river/ Men may come and men may go but I go on forever'.

One of Frith's pictures taken in 1913 shows two boys with the Town Mill in the background looking down into the river where trout tend to gather. Today, raising their heads, they would no doubt be amused to see the representation of the Viking Longboat about to depart down the river. Whatever the changes, the view would still be recognised. Directly opposite them, they would certainly recognise the ramp into the ford from the yard of the Bell Inn in the High Street by which coaches and wagons heading west would have crossed the water to Bridge Street.

Until 1964, Bridge Street would normally have been the place where train travellers stepped into the town, and it is here that Frith's pictures take over as guide around Andover and some of the nearby villages.

The name of Longparish is worth a special mention: this was the name adopted in the late 19th century to unite four ancient tithings into a single community, stretching three miles along the road which follows the Test, from Hurstbourne Priors to the London to Exeter trunk route.

Of the area around Andover, some interesting folk tales survive. For instance, it is said that a toad hatched a duck egg in Wherwell Priory crypt. The fierce creature which emerged grew to be enormous, with razor-sharp talons and breathing fire, and killed all who came near it. The nuns

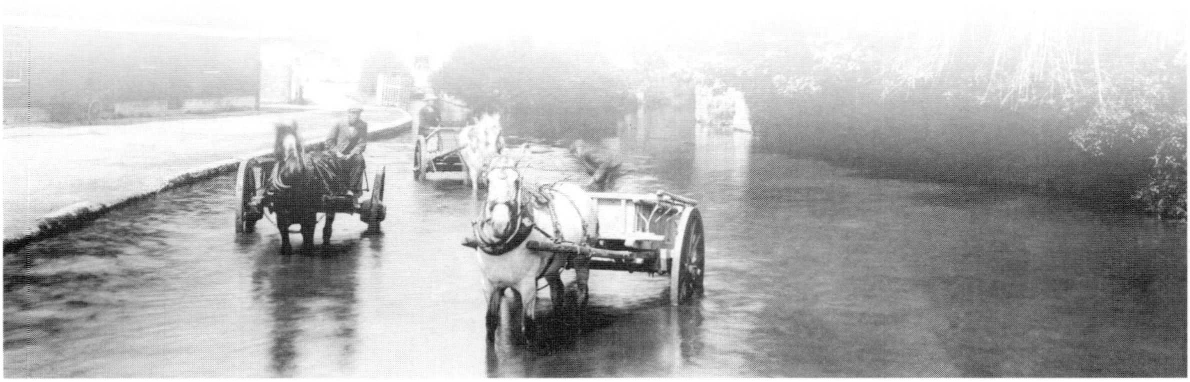

cowered in terror. Fearing it would break out to attack them all, the villagers fed it whole sheep, which only added to its size and ferocity. One villager, Green, ingenious and braver than the others, held a polished steel shield within the vault. The beast was so enraged by its reflection that it exhausted itself in its furious attack upon the image. Green gamely entered the crypt and cut off its head. His reward was a plot in Harewood Forest, still known as Green's Acre. And that is why, to this day, no one in Wherwell eats duck eggs!

Finally, the Legend of Elfrida. In 963, Edgar the Peacemaker sent Ethelwold to see if Princess Elfrida, daughter of King Orgar of Devon, was as beautiful as reputed. Ethelwold was so smitten by her charms that he decided to marry her himself and took her home to Wherwell. 'She is plain', he artfully told the King. In due course, while hunting near Wherwell, the King saw Elfrida and, realising that he had been duped, led Ethelwold deep into Harewood Forest. There he ran his lance through his faithless emissary and took the lady himself. In 1825 a tall Saxon cross of stone on an inscribed base was erected to mark the reputed spot of the foul deed. It stands to this day on Dead Man's Plack.

The following scenes, photographed over the past 150 years or so, continue to be highly recognisable, despite the many changes that have taken place. As a collection, they enrich our understanding of the town and add depth in a very real way.

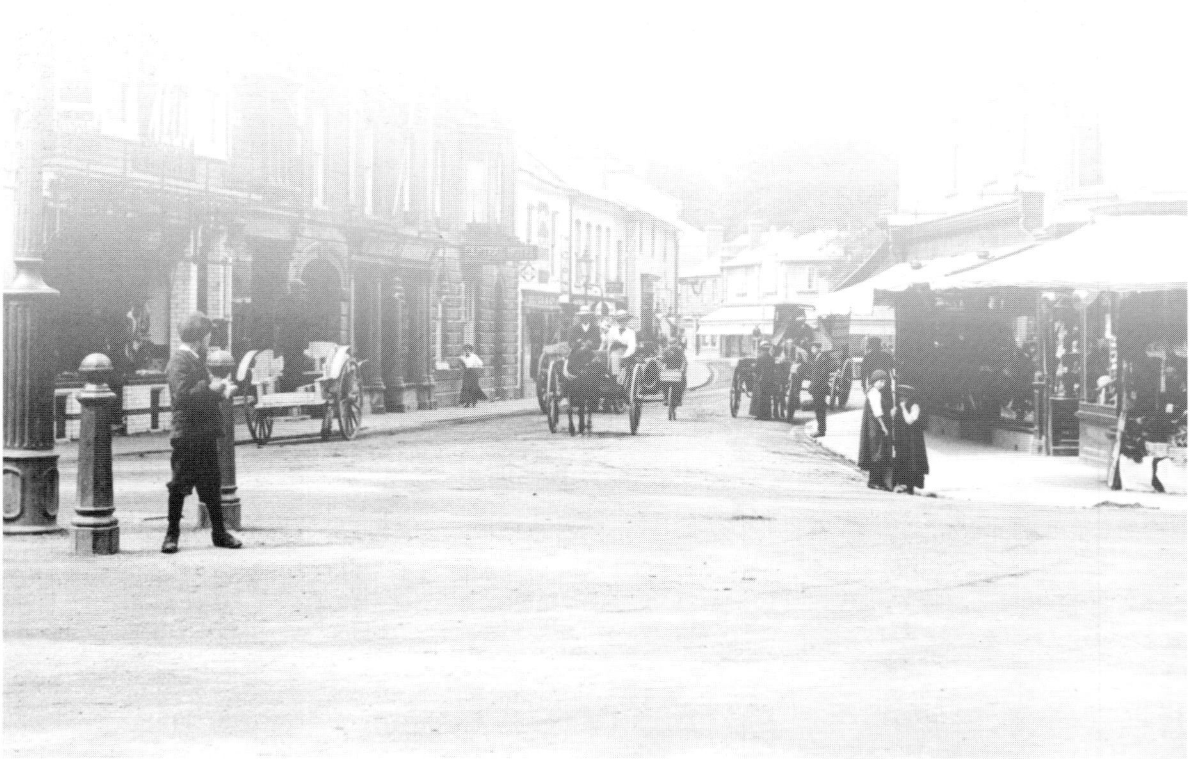

Town Station and Bridge Street

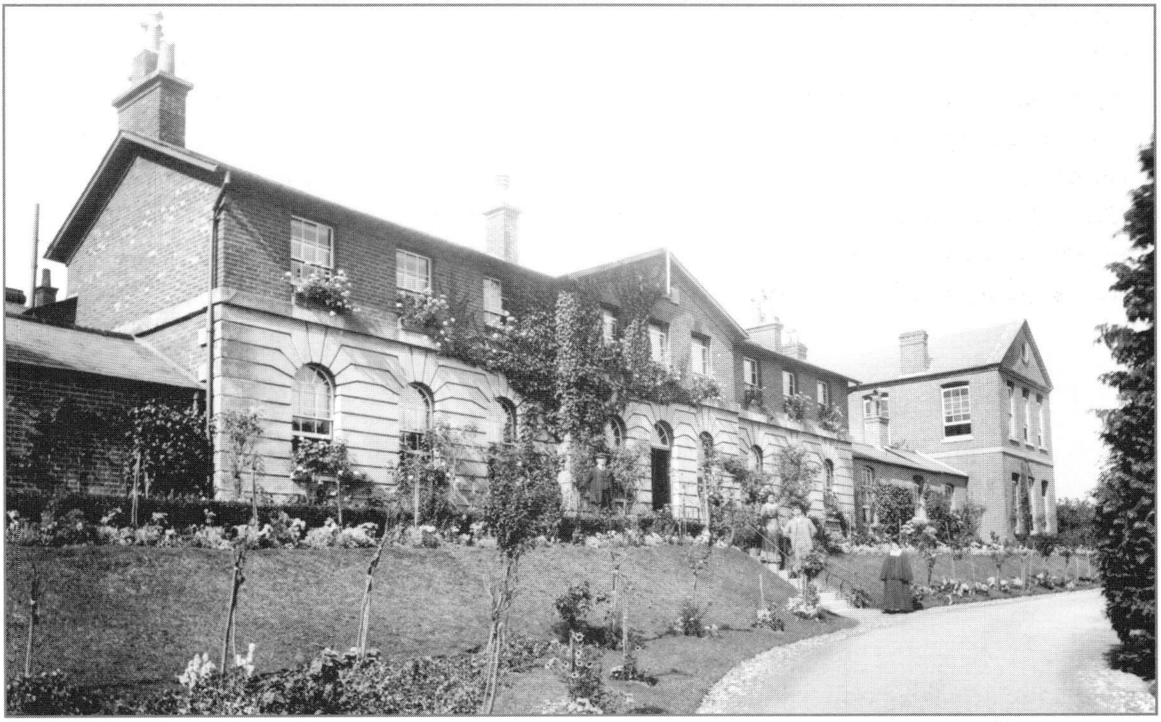

Union Workhouse, Junction Road 1906 54627
Having opened in 1836, the Union offered a harsh regime until the abolition of the Poor Law in 1929. In 1948, St John's Hospital for the aged and infirm came on site. A girls' hostel was added in 1972, and sheltered housing for the elderly was built in 1982. That year the hospital moved to Charlton Road and Cricklade College took over the workhouse as classrooms. From 1998 the old buildings were converted to private flats, and by 2001 a large number of private houses and flats had been built for sale on the rest of the site.

▼ The Round House 1898 42086

The road divides at this toll house, heading to Salisbury to the left and Ludgershall to the right. Trusts usually ran at a loss, but the Andover Turnpike Trust from Basingstoke to Lopcombe Corner was uniquely profitable thanks to Hampshire's stable and well-drained chalk. The turnpike closed in 1872, and the building came down in the 1930s.

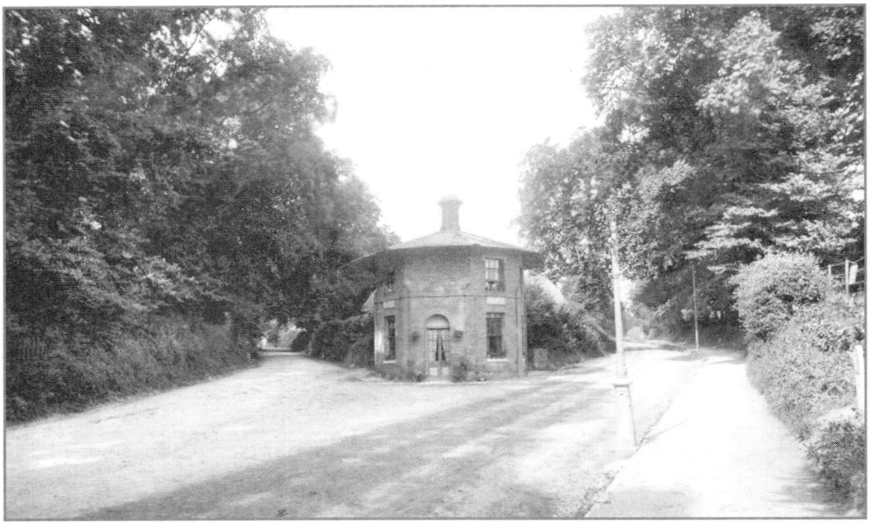

▼ The Town Station and Level Crossing 1908 60096

These passengers have just alighted from a train out of Southampton. See the signal box beside the level crossing and fine old gas lamps to the right. Lord Beeching closed this branch line in 1964. Its 22-mile length became a track known as the Test Way, which can now be walked from Andover all the way to Southampton Water.

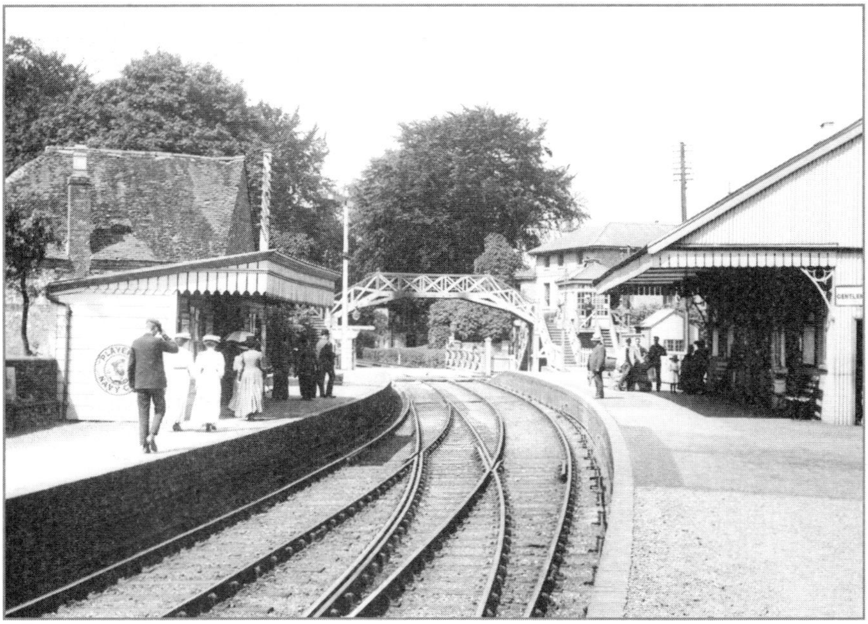

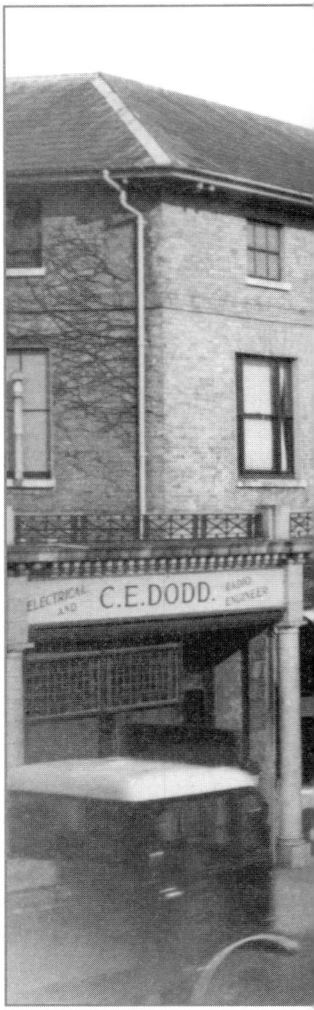

▲ Bridge Street from the Level Crossing 1939 A49011

By 1939 the level crossing was so busy that during rush hours there would frequently be a bottleneck on the main road to the west. Buildings opposite the signal box have all gone, but some shops and the Post Office with its domed cupola still remain.

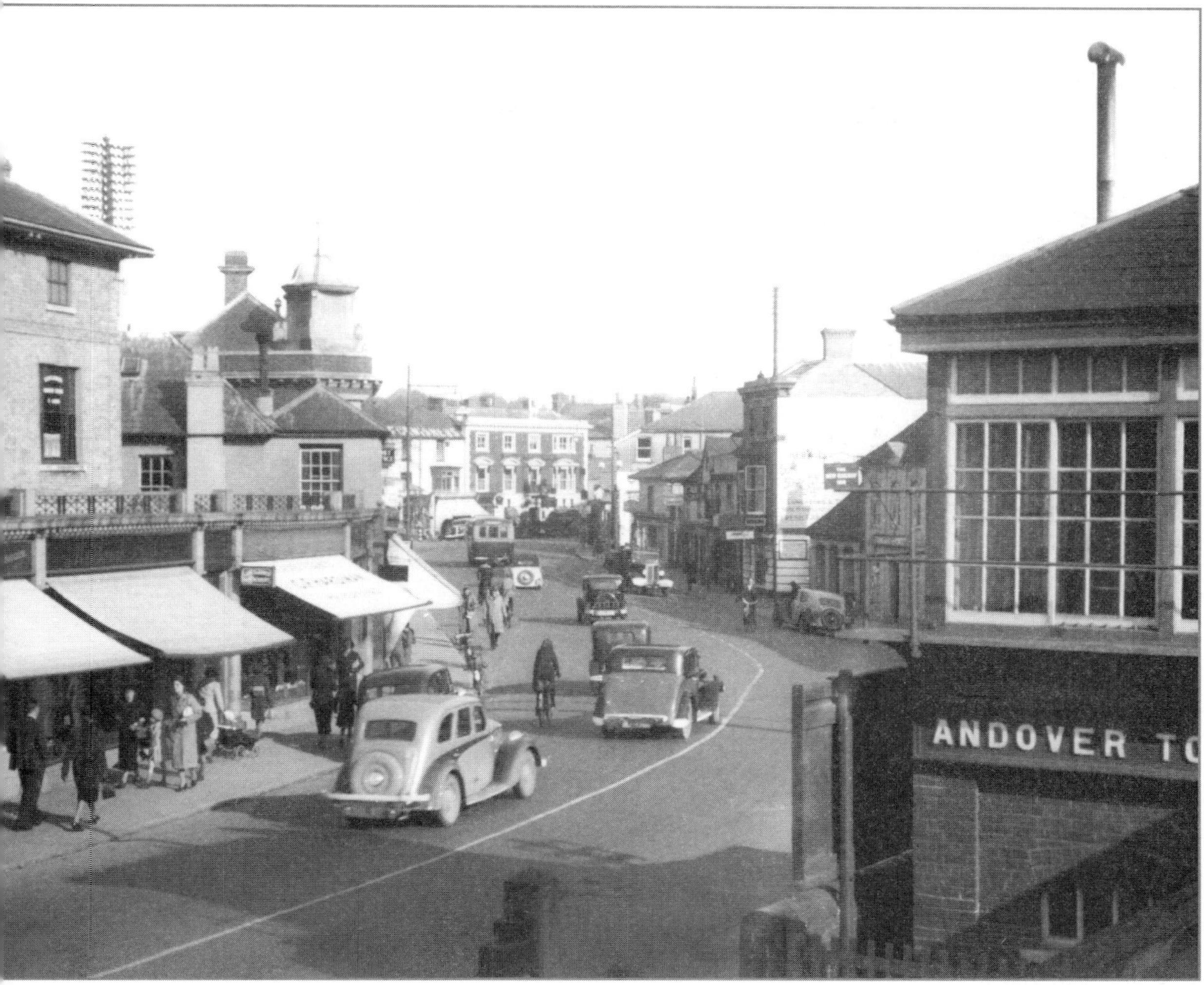

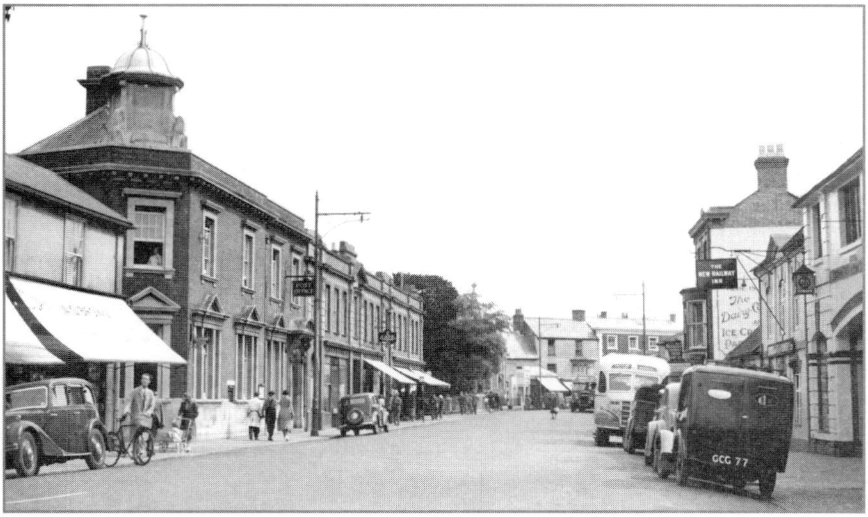

◄ **Bridge Street and the Post Office c1950** A49041

In 1950 people going to or from the station would also be shopping. Built in the 1920s, the Co-op had its own café. Across the road were two others. The Bedford bus would leave from here for Amport. Just visible on the right, Henly's Garage was redeveloped in 1982 for Safeway. The New Railway Inn later became a shop with an arcade behind. A O Brown, Watchmaker & Jeweller, became Sally Ann's in 2001.

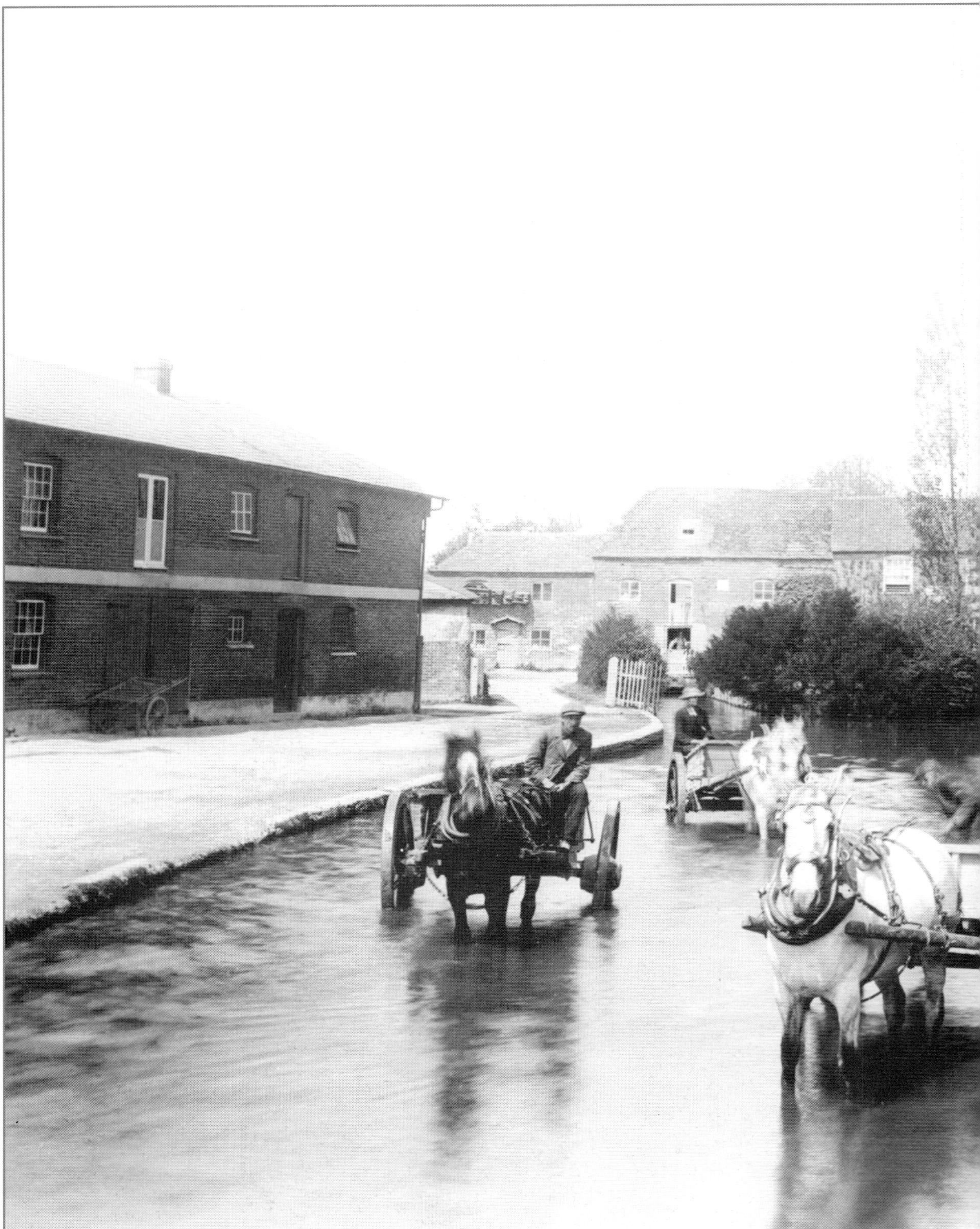

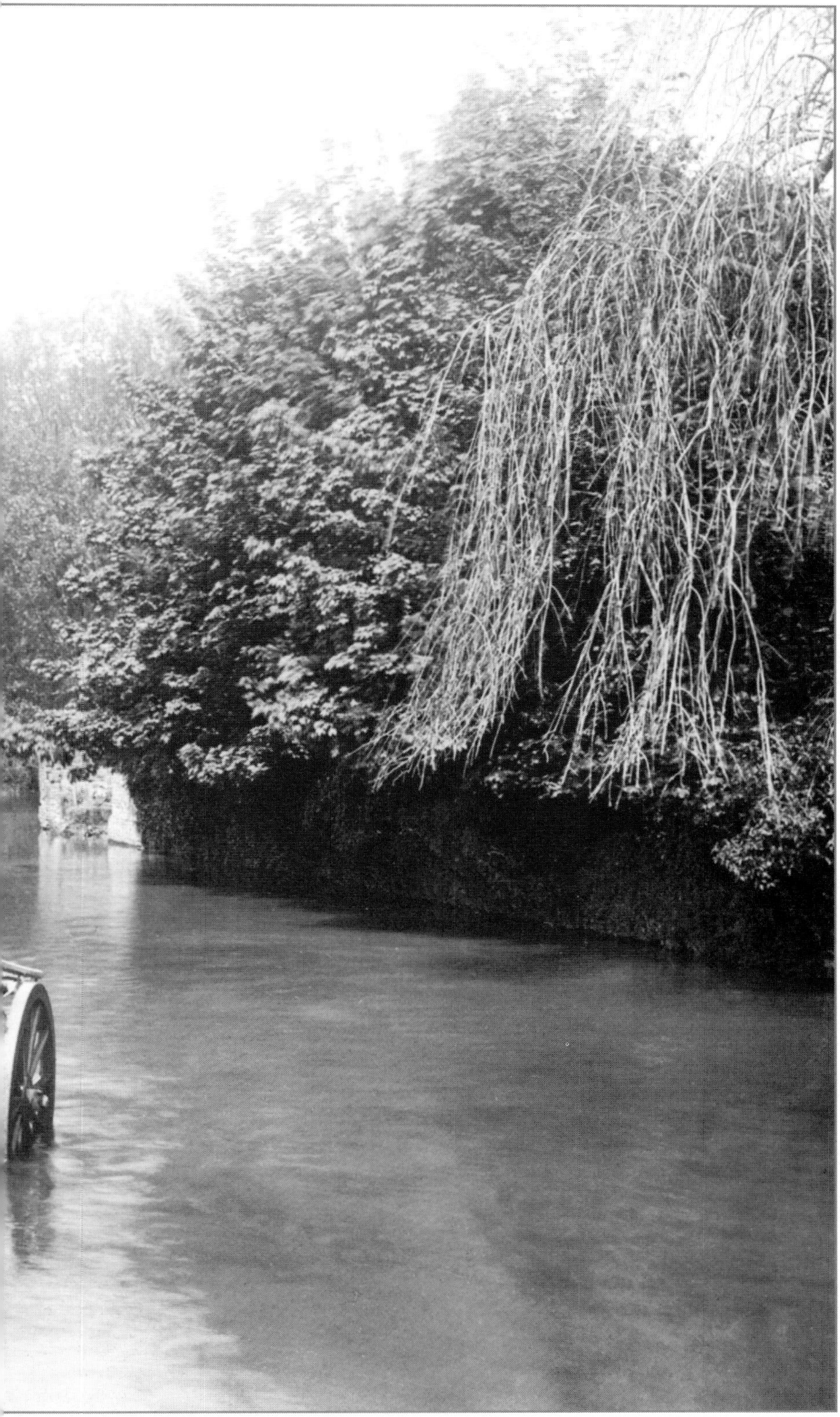

The Town River 1901
46351
Before the Town Bridge was strengthened, heavy carts had to ford the river from either the ramp at the sunlit break beyond the trees or another ramp on the right beside the bridge.

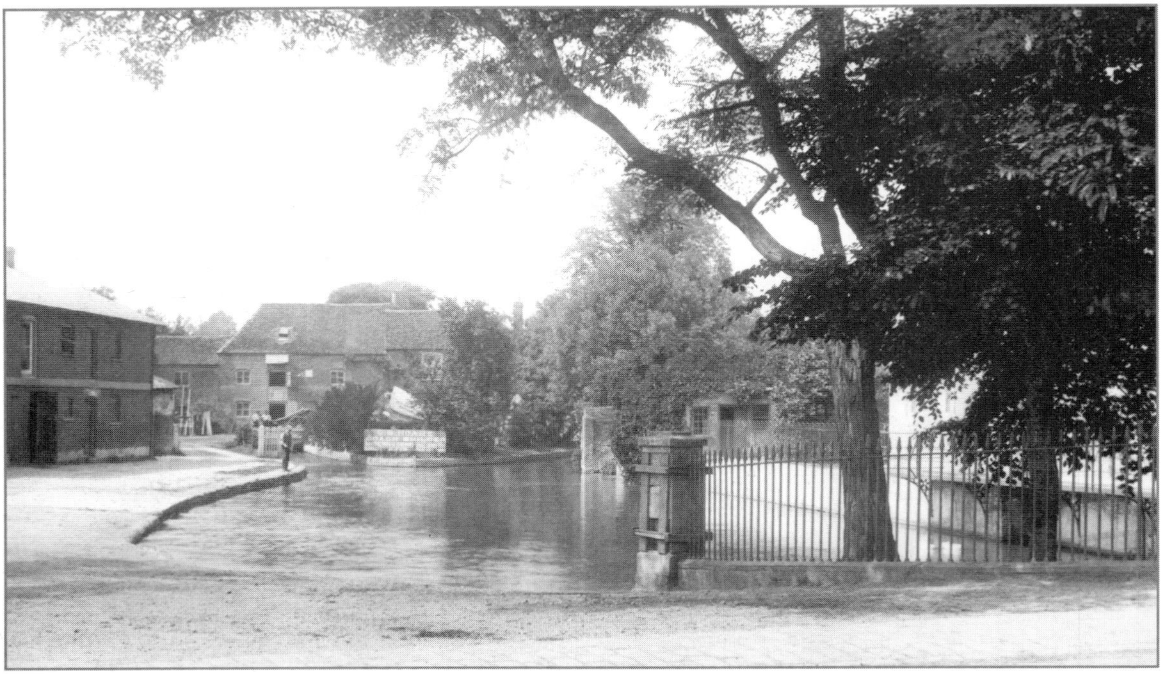

The Town Mill 1908 60095
Seen from the west ramp of the ford, G H Hoare, Coach Building, Shoeing & General Smith, advertises his work, while a man fishes below the island where brown trout still swim against the flow.

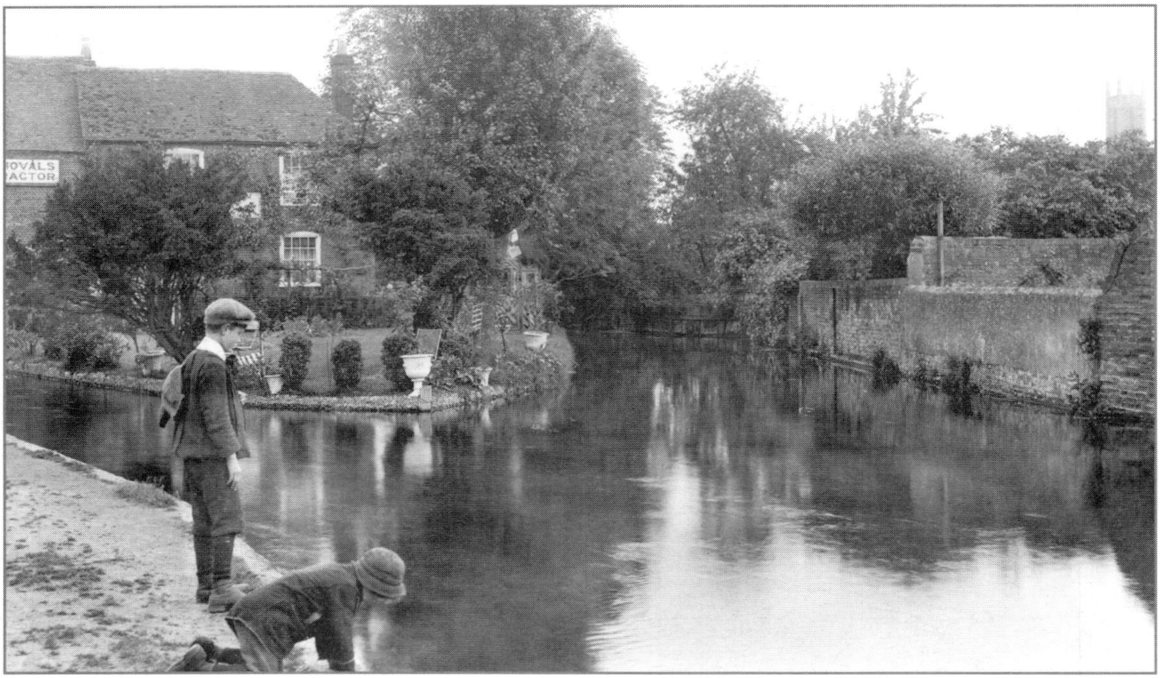

The Town Mill 1913 65318
In this picture, the mill owner's garden has been much improved since Mr Hoare's advertisement hoarding has been tidied away.

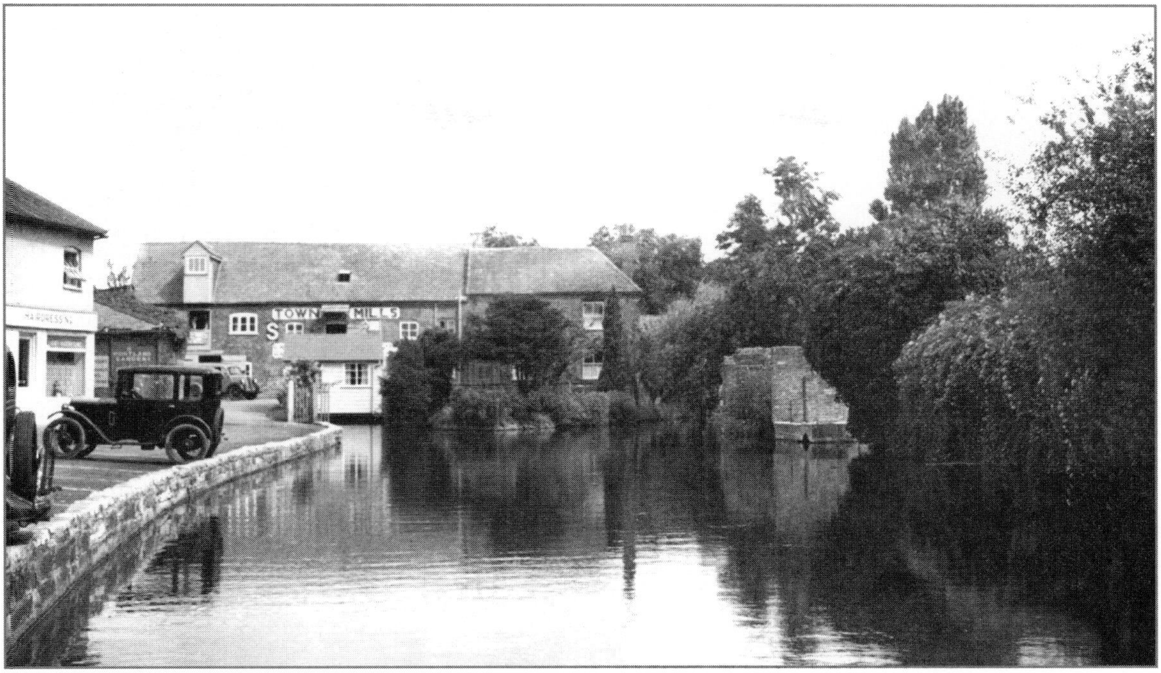

The River and Town Mill c1950 A49038
After the Second World War, old cars came back on the road and new production increased. The edge of the river was soon marked out for free parking. Note the hut spanning the mill race.

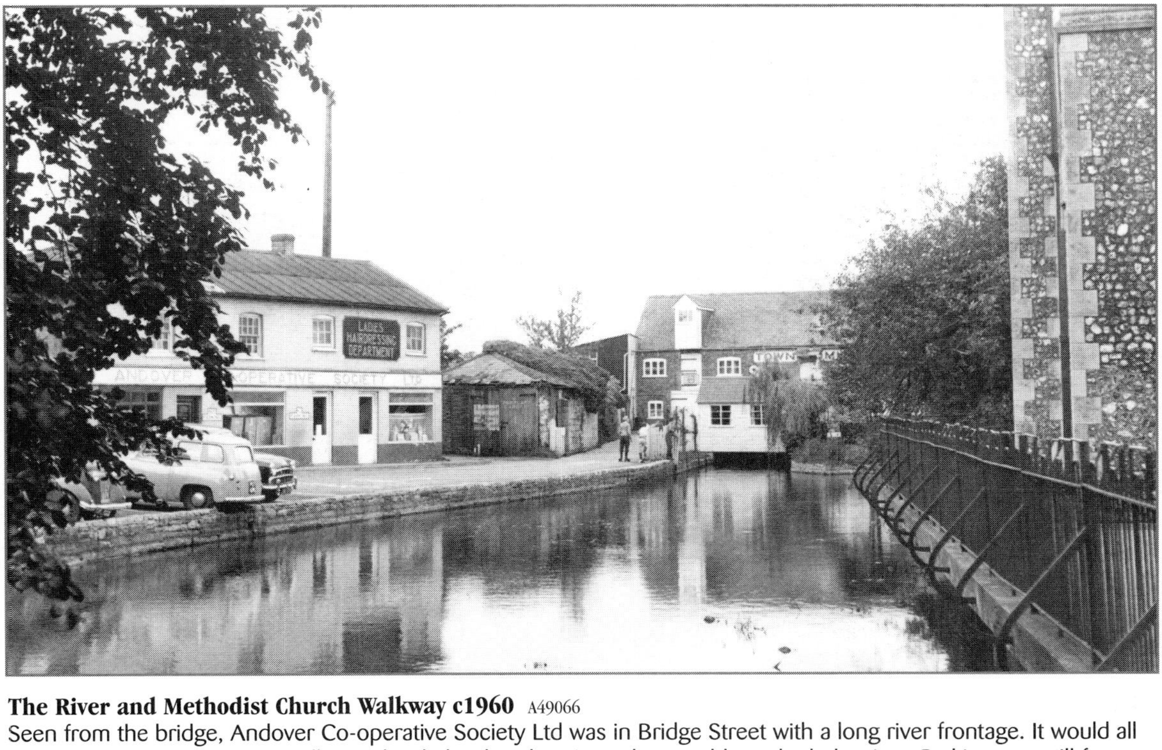

The River and Methodist Church Walkway c1960 A49066
Seen from the bridge, Andover Co-operative Society Ltd was in Bridge Street with a long river frontage. It would all be rebuilt about 1970. Eventually another ladies hairdressing salon would overlook the river. Parking was still free.

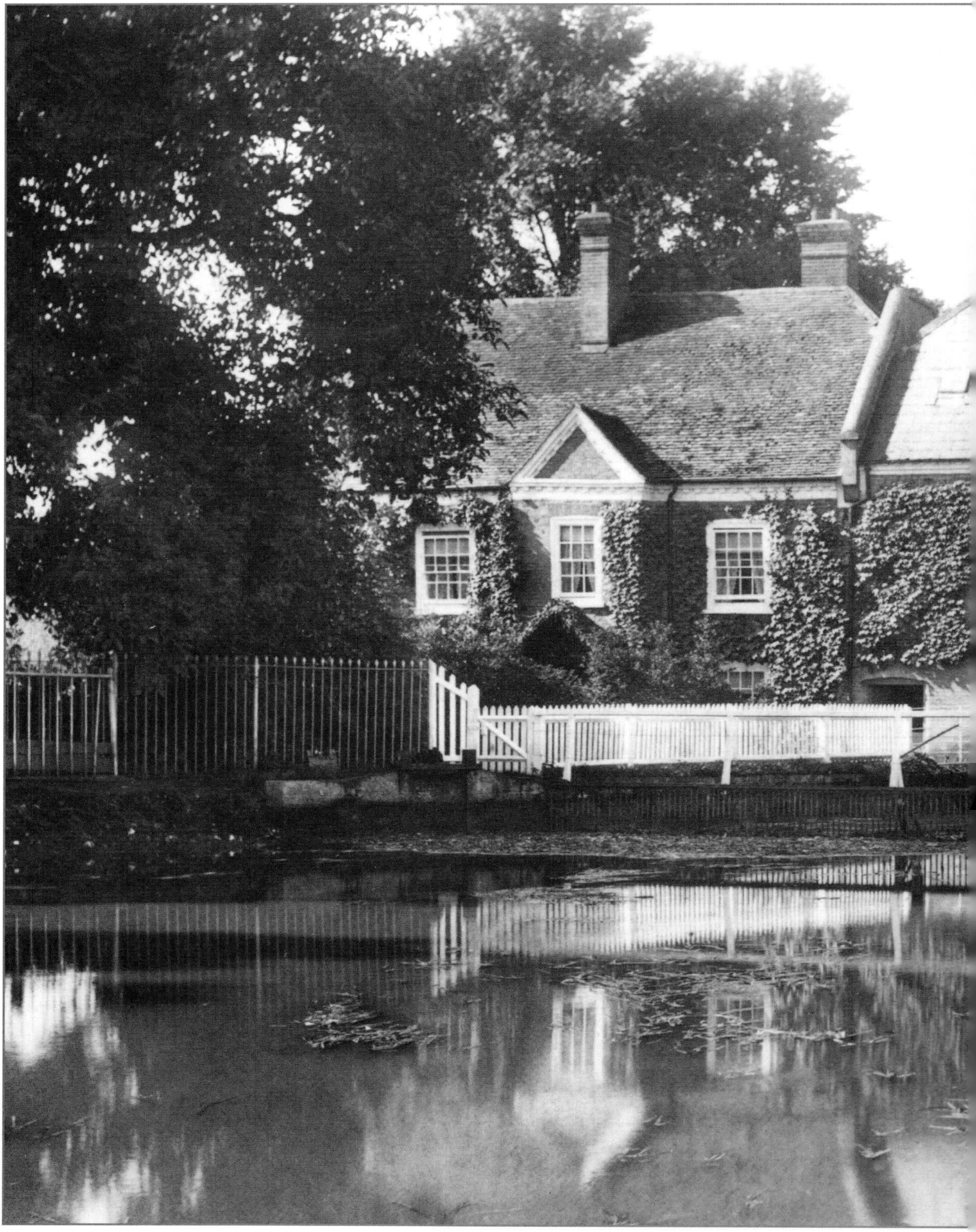

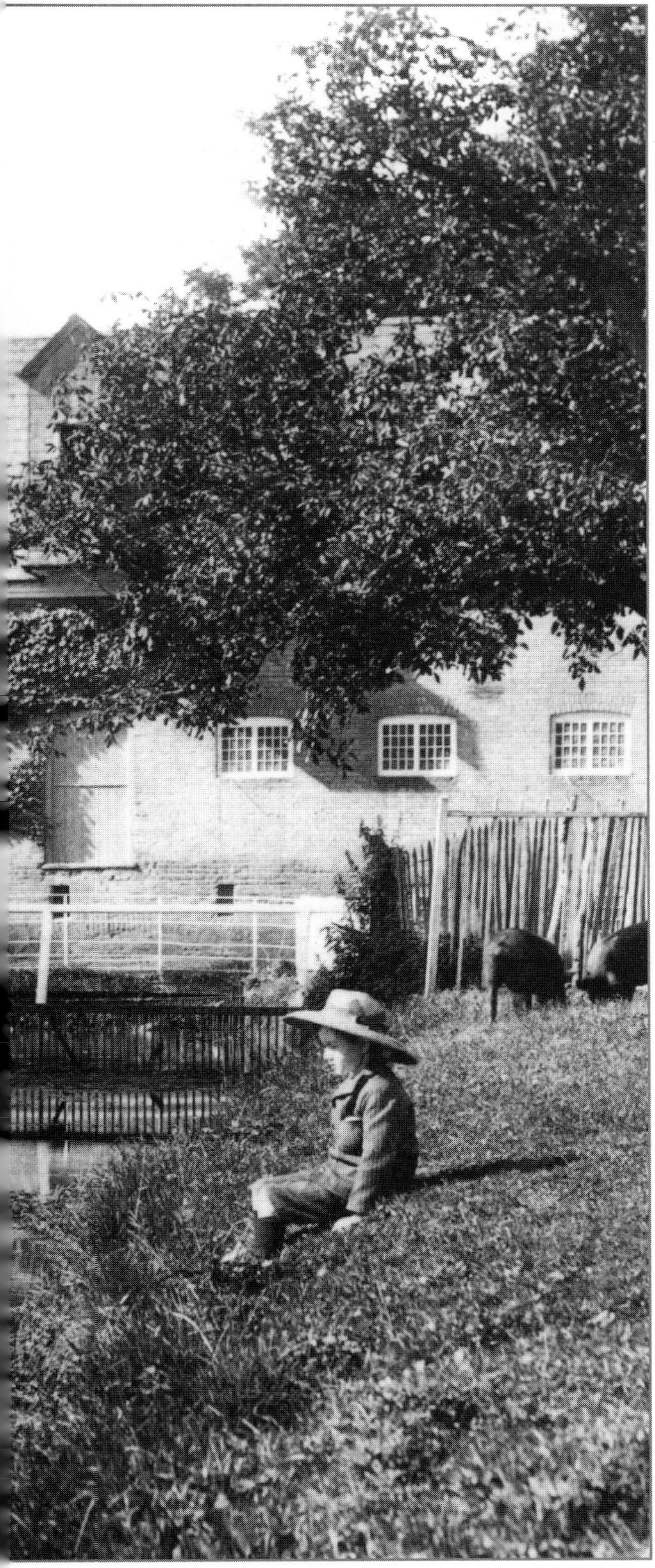

A Diversion to Rooksbury Mill

Anton Mill 1906 54631
In this picture, Anton Mill, some distance down-river beside Barlows Lane, can be compared with the Town Mill. This pleasant Georgian building was taken over by Hovis in 1914. Flour milling was run down; by 1953, the production was animal feed. In the early 1960s the mill was demolished and the site redeveloped by Locomotors to produce security and other special vehicles, but Frith's fine picture remains.

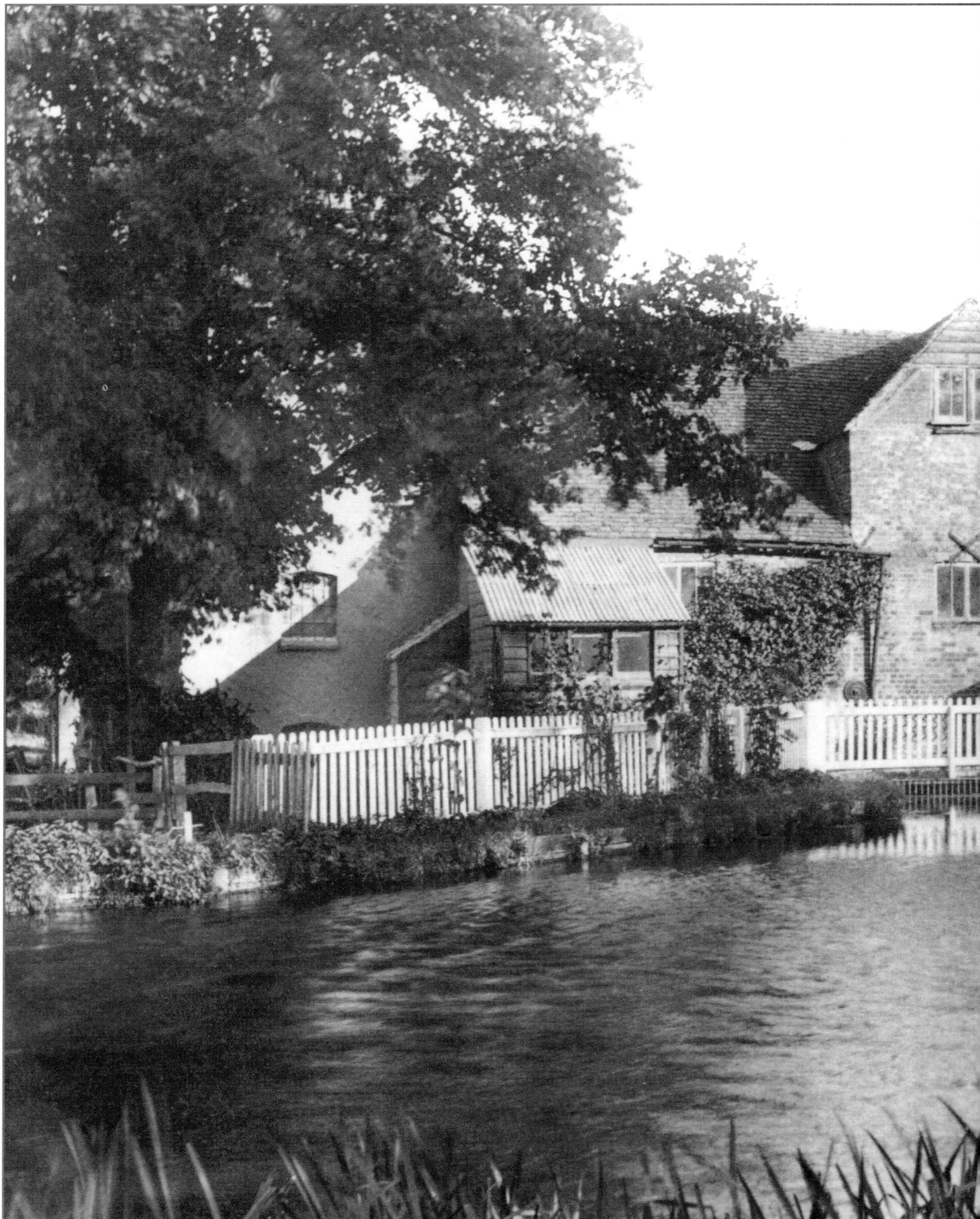

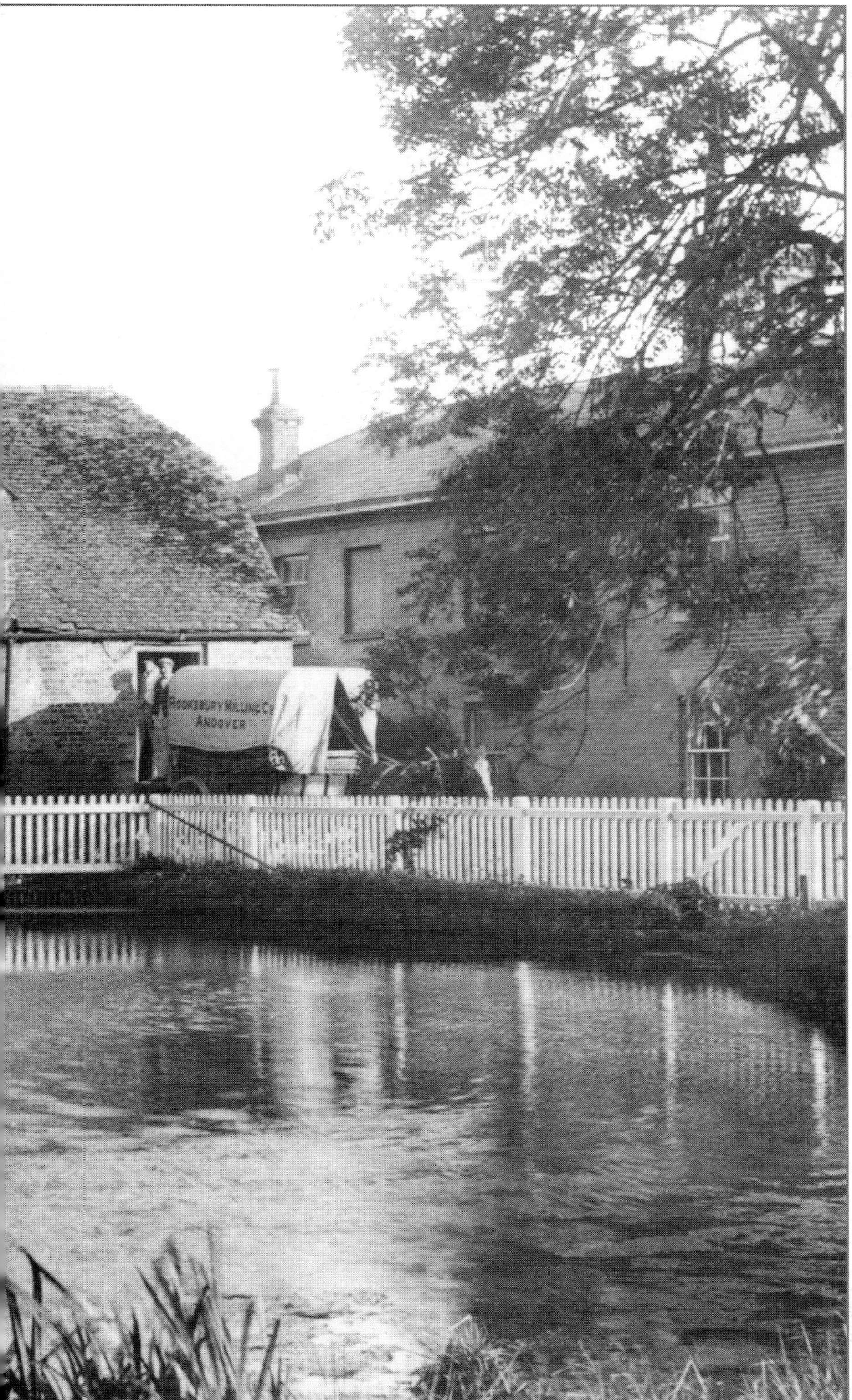

Rooksbury Mill 1906 54632
Further down-river, Rooksbury Mill stands on the edge of town as the only other mill still existing. In 2001 the Council bought Rooksbury Mill and its use as a fisherman's club may change.

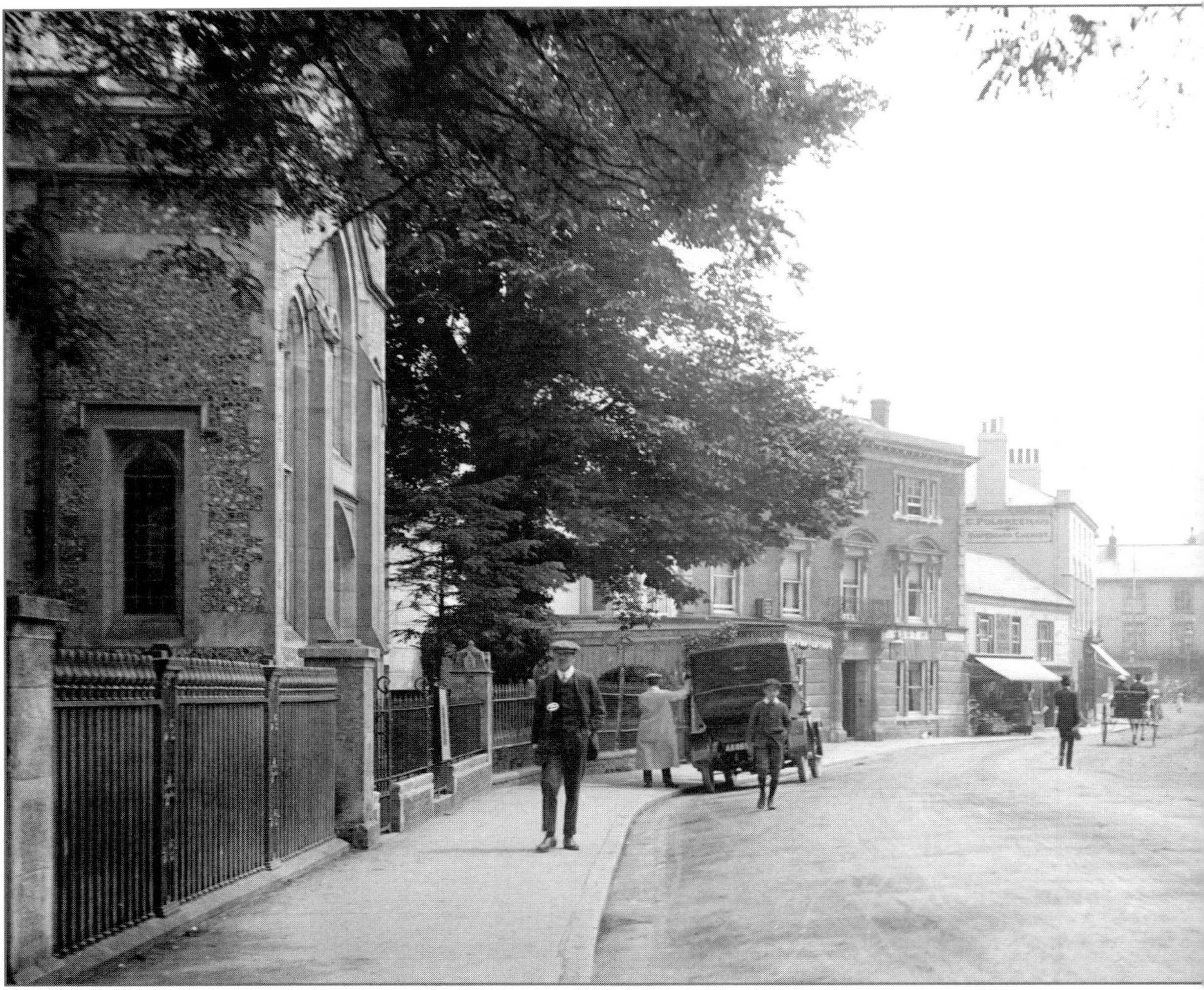

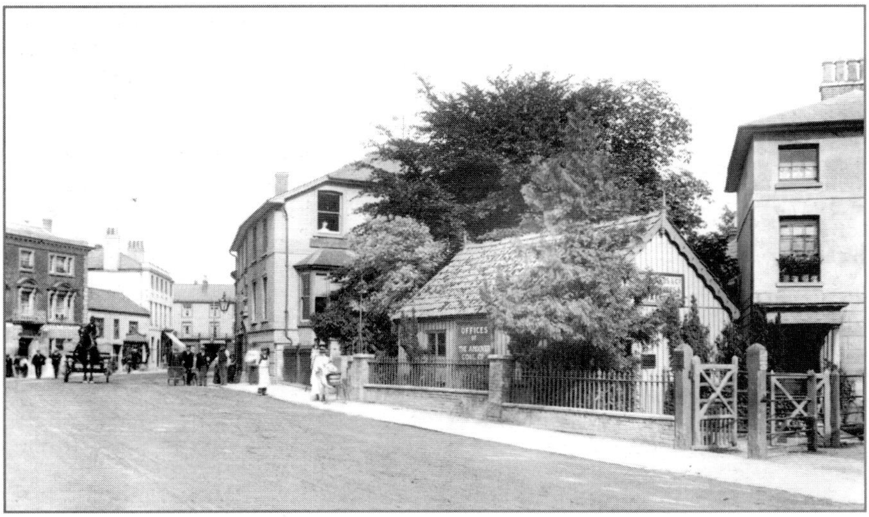

◀ **Bridge Street 1904**

52145

Before 1865 in Andover, coal had been unloaded on the canal basin quay. By 1904 the quay had gone and larger quantities of heavy goods were being handled on the railway sidings, which had replaced the canal basin. Here by the bridge was the office of the Andover Coal Company.

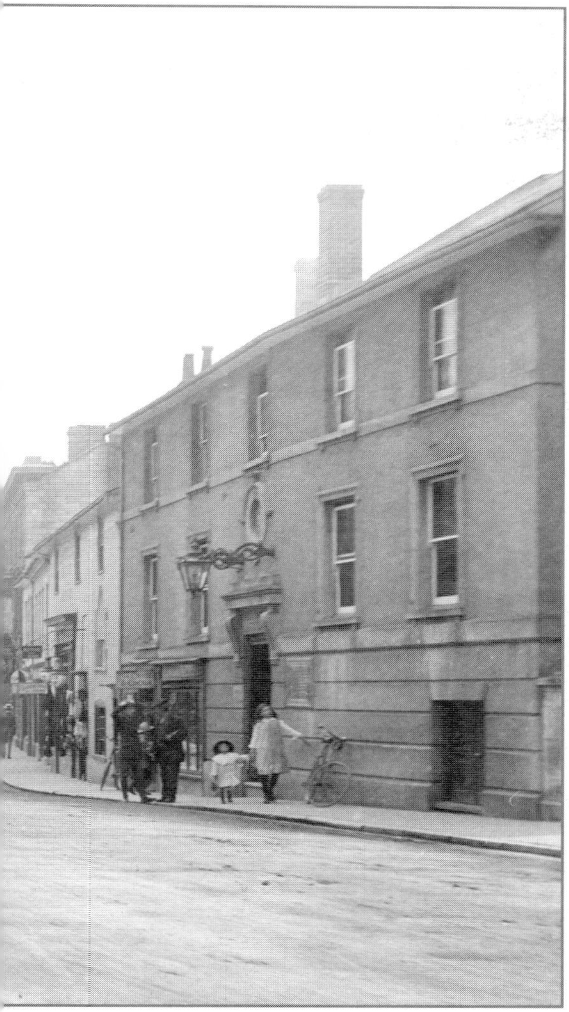

Return to Bridge Street and Town

Bridge Street 1913 65316
The bridge was not always as level, strong and wide as this. In 1758 the old bridge was restricted to pedestrians and horses by a bar and lamp directing wagons and coaches behind the railings into the ford. When a strong bridge was built, the ford became redundant; the Methodist Church has stood there on the ramp since 1905.

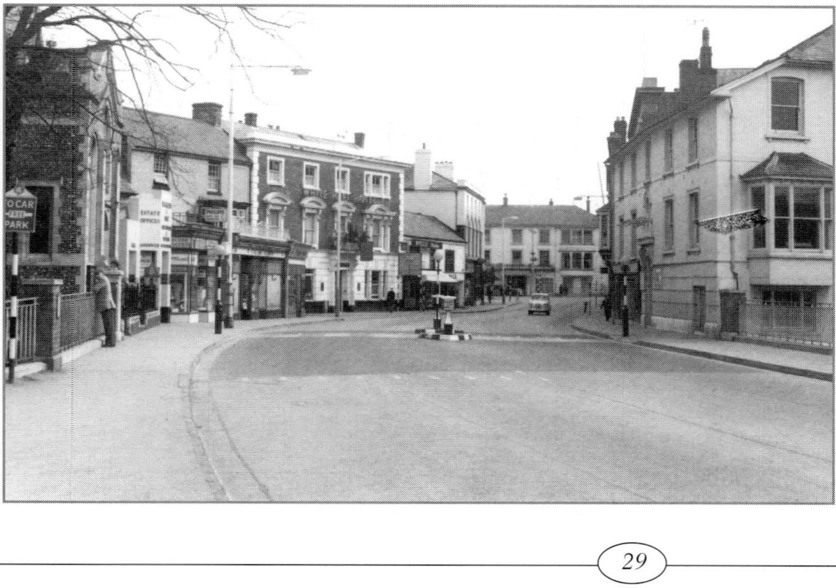

Bridge Street c1960 A49084
A man leans on the bridge rail beside the Methodist Church. Next door, Frank May, Auctioneer and Estate Agent, is now Redwoods. A lone Austin A35 has the street to itself, while the door of the Star and Garter is still locked tight. On the right is the Free Public Library, the Art School above and Florabunda's flowers below. General Shubrick's clock over the door came from the Round House when the Andover Turnpike Trust was wound up.

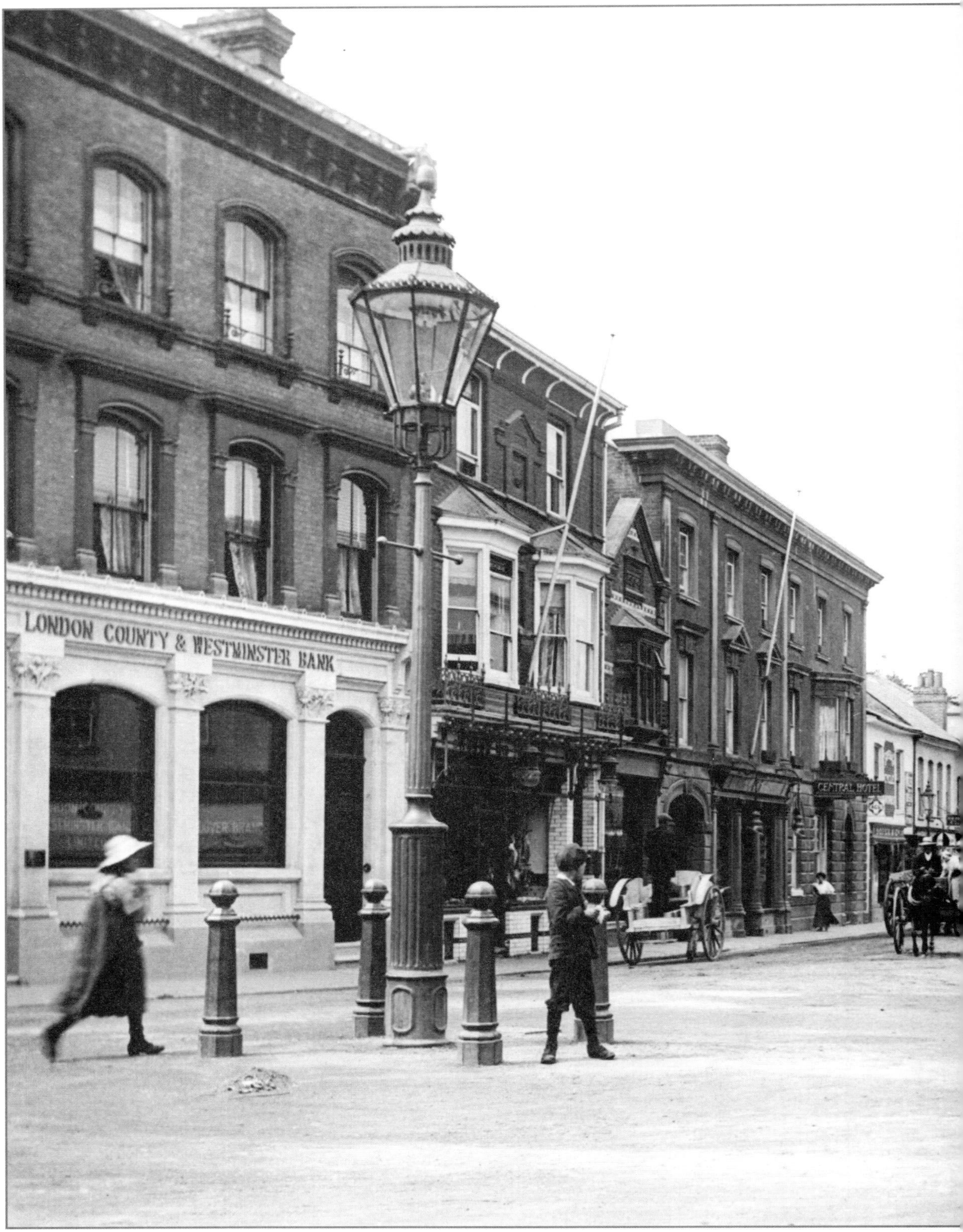
LONDON COUNTY & WESTMINSTER BANK
CENTRAL HOTEL

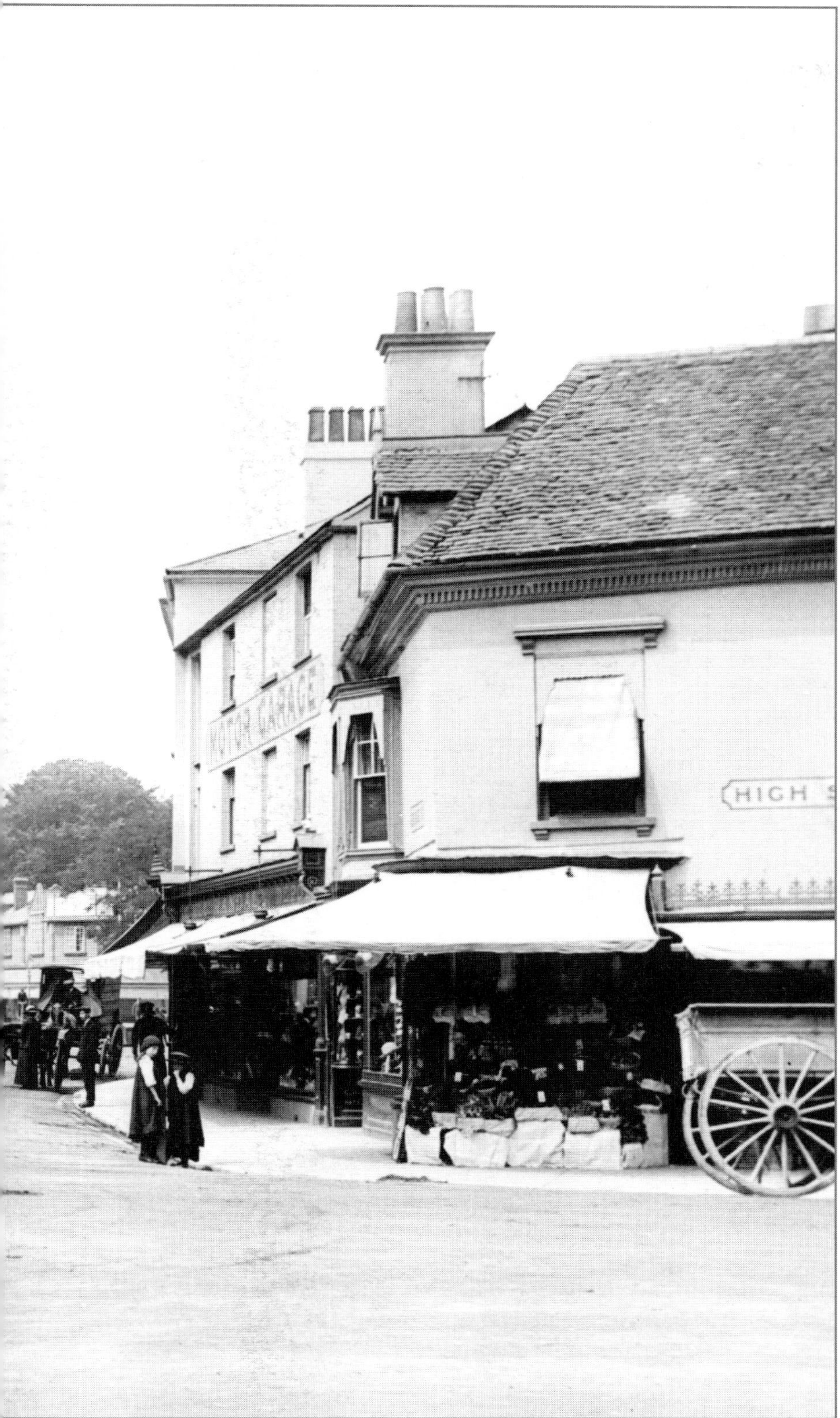

Bridge Street 1913
65317
Looking back into Bridge Street at Burden's Corner, the London County & Westminster Bank retained its authentic late Victorian frontage. Andover Lighting and Power, in the small gabled building built in 1904, disappeared with neighbouring Central Hotel. Their sites were redeveloped in the 1960s. Between the motor garage and the corner were Pullar's of Perth, Dyers and Cleaners.

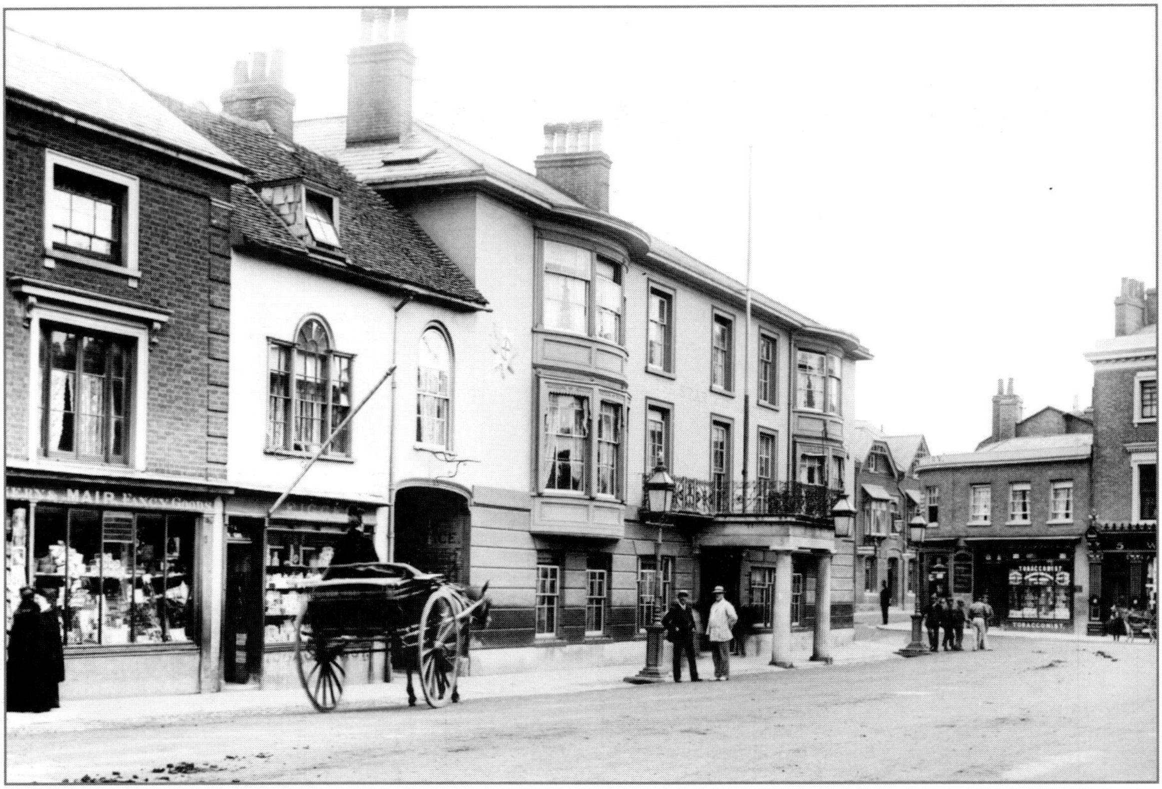

High Street 1904 52149

The smart Danebury Hotel, at this time called the Star and Garter, has changed little over the years. The coach arch still leads to Star Yard at the back.

Andover Lower High Street to the Angel Inn

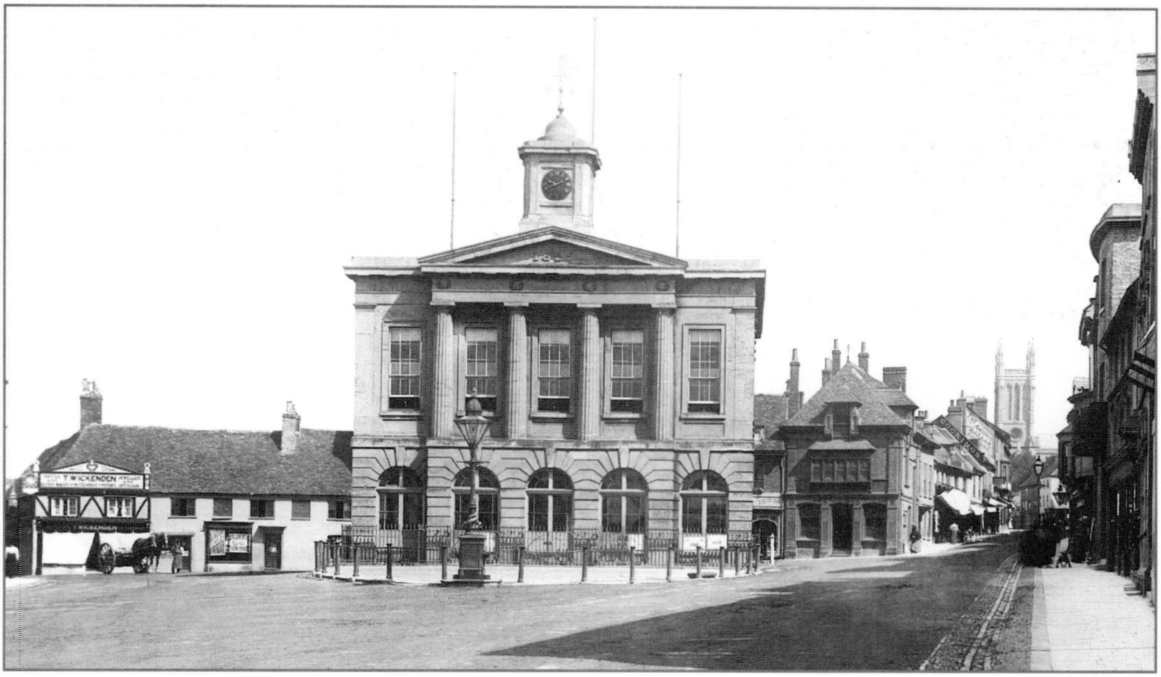

The Guildhall and High Street 1898 42081
The original Guildhall was Elizabethan - this picture shows the fine Palladian replacement of 1825 with its Regency cupola and clock. The cupola was removed in 1904 as the roof was sagging. Tasker's gas lamp, erected for Queen Victoria's Golden Jubilee of 1887, went into storage in 1919, making way for the Cenotaph which in turn was moved to St Mary's Parish Church in 1956. The lamp has recently been returned to the forecourt.

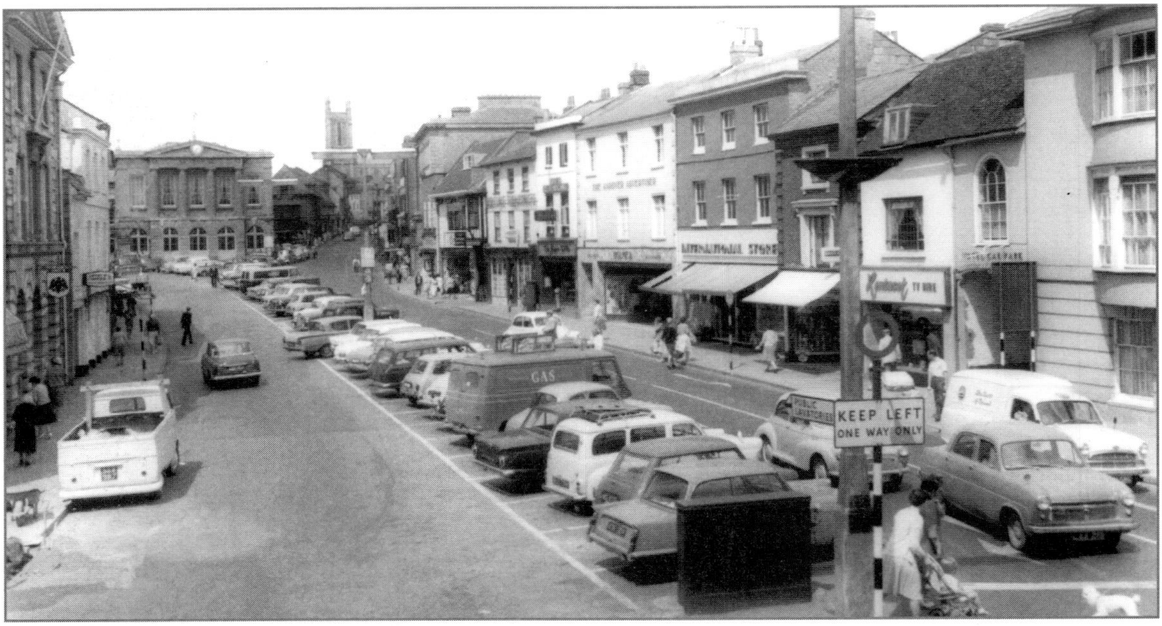

High Street c1960 A49094
The Guildhall still dominates this scene of the lower High Street. Cars fill a single line of parking on the waste of the manor. The pavement is up and men are busy in front of Burden's shop. Tea could be had next door to Barclays Bank or in the Copper Kettle across the road, by Holmes & Sons, printers of the Andover Advertiser. The premises were sold in 2001 to become a Wetherspoon hostelry. Paper production would move to London Street after more than 144 years.

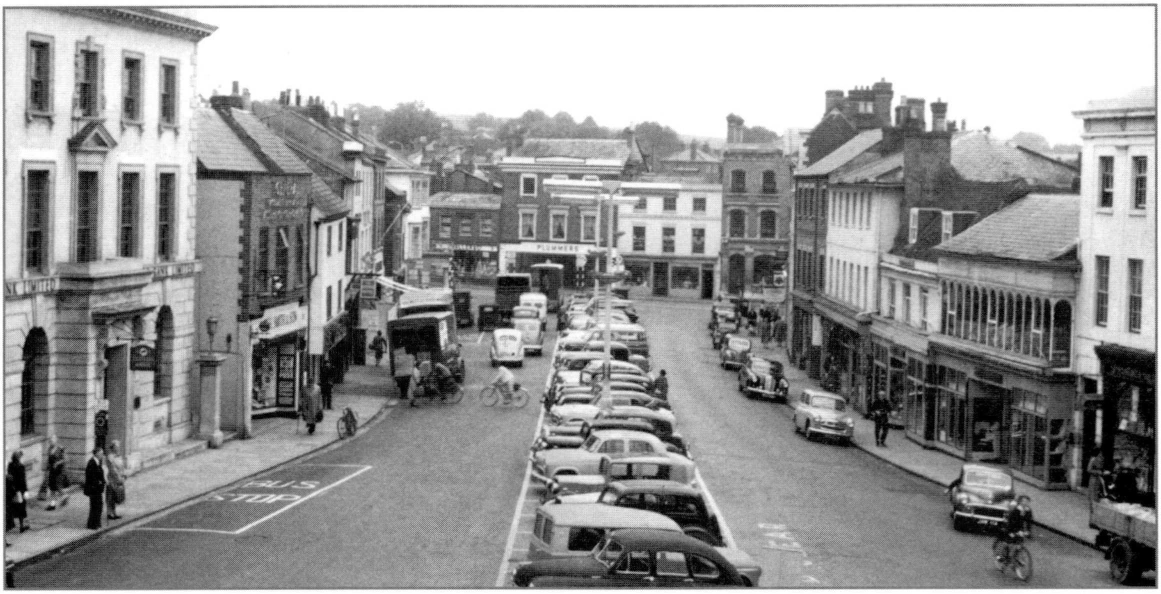

High Street c1955 A49069
This view is from an upper floor window in the Guildhall. Woolworths has yet to appear on the right, in place of Parsons and Hart's three buildings - it was to break the Victorian rhythm of shopfronts. Plummers were still in the High Street in the 1960s. Next to Lloyds Bank, W H Smith has long since given way to C & M DIY. There is talk in 2001 of upgrading the market street for the comfort of the silent majority, the town's pedestrians.

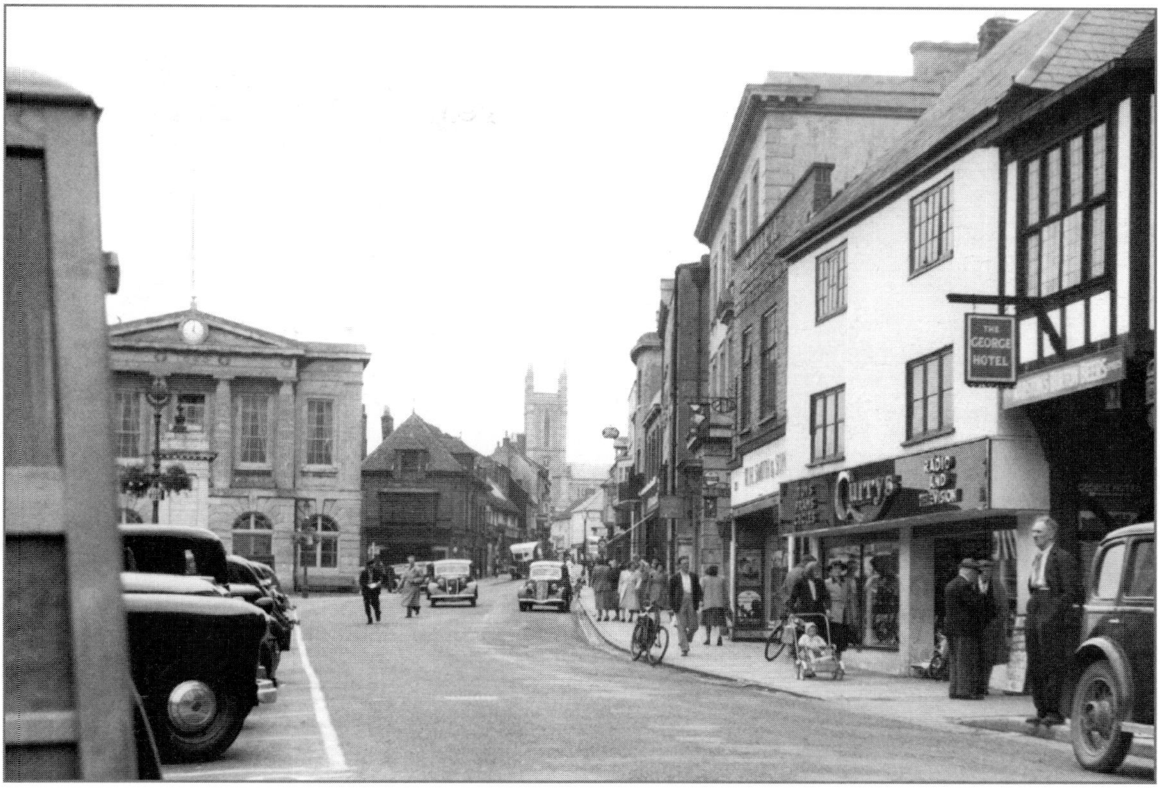

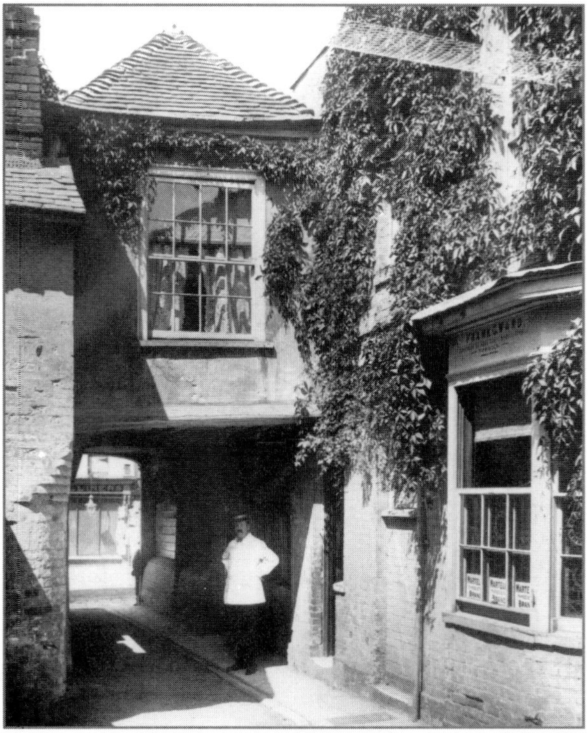

High Street c1950 A49030

The George Hotel is entered through the old coaching arch under a 20th-century leaded window. From 1586 an Elizabethan inn thrived here as one of Andover's larger coaching inns, but now, through the arch, only the Georgian rebuild of the hotel remains, with hardly a yard and nothing of the stables.

The George Hotel 1908 60097

In 1768, Sir Francis Blake Delaval, canvassing for election as MP, and his agent Kellynge invited the Mayor and Corporation and the Colonel and Officers of a local billet to a grand dinner. Mayhem ensued when it came to paying the bill, for each party believed itself the guest of the other. The colonel threw Kellynge out of the window, and the latter sued Sir Francis for £500 for a broken leg, the surgeon's bill, and the loss of time and business!

▼ **High Street c1960** A49078

The buildings behind the Guildhall would soon be replaced as part of the agreement with Greater London Council, which would more than double the town's population in less than twenty years.

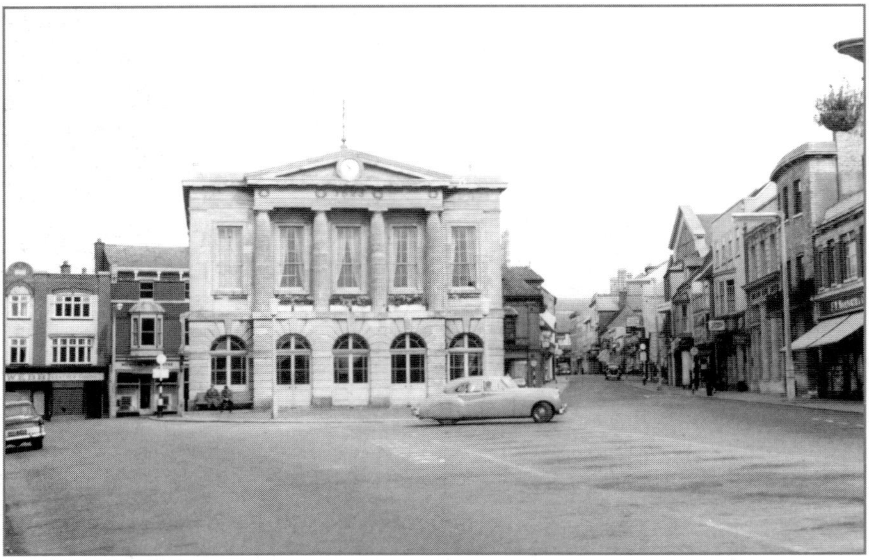

▼ **High Street c1955** A49064

In the 1970s double-decker buses passed in the upper High Street. People on busy pavements feared for their safety, a sure case for pedestrianisation.

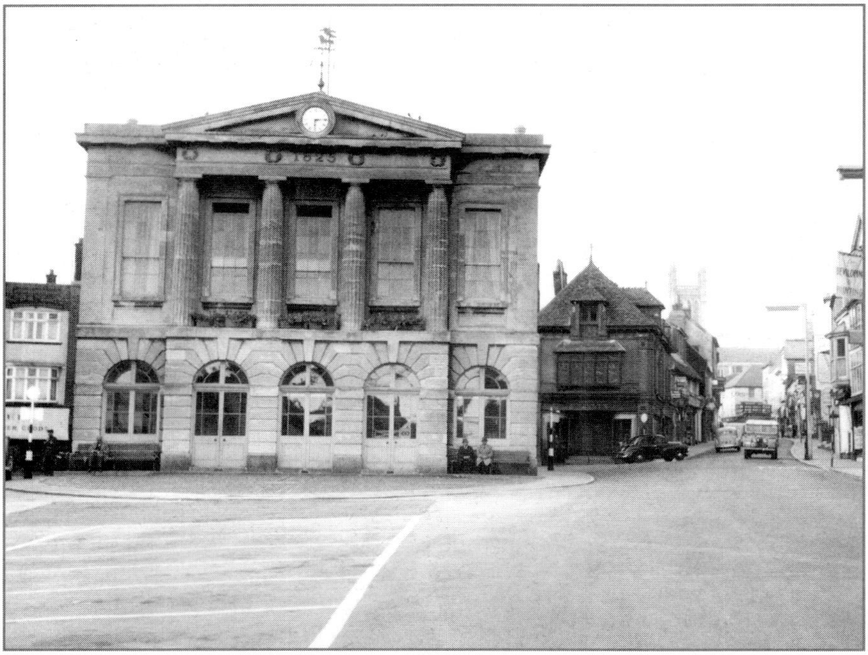

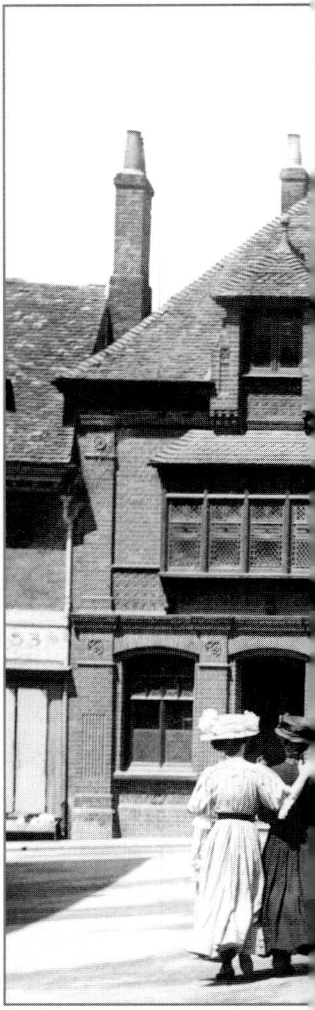

▲ **High Street 1908** 60092

This Edwardian picture would make a fine backdrop to an Andover stage production. Poore's Victorian brewery office became Handel House around 1920, with a wide altered shop-front selling pianos, followed soon after by A B Scott's shoe shop. Even now, the loss of Scott's Corner is lamented. Although gone forever, such detail remains in Frith's picture as could still be copied elsewhere.

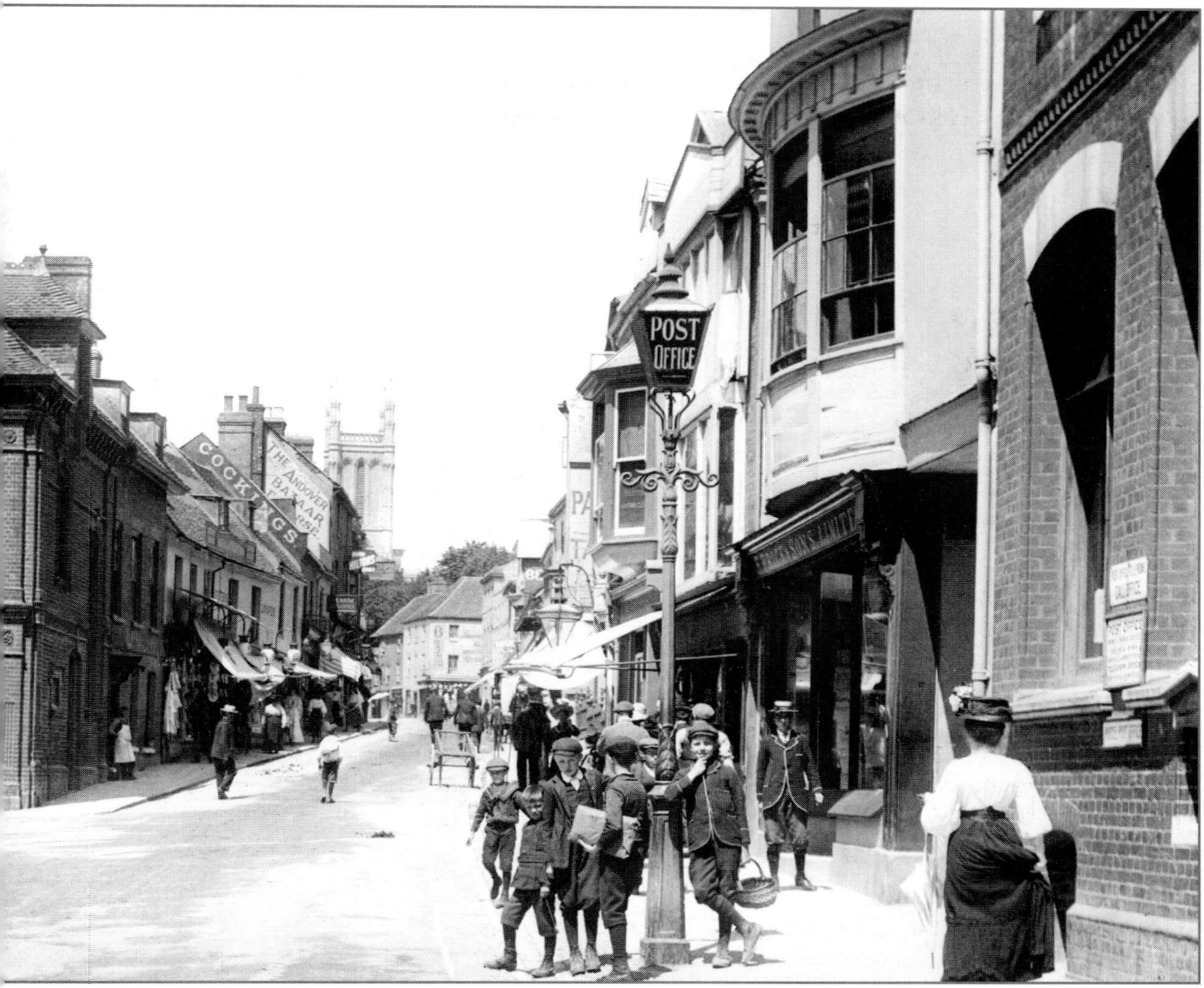

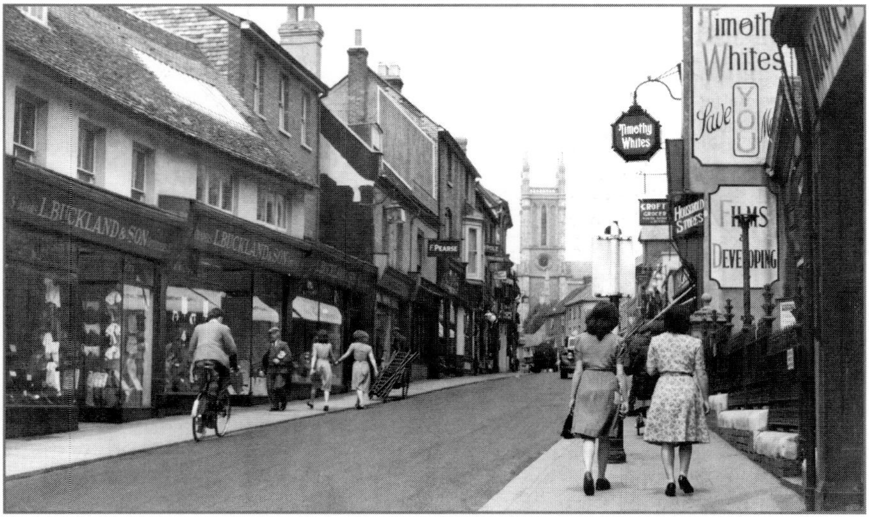

High Street c1950 A49020

The cyclist passes Buckland & Son, Tailors and Outfitters, an old fashioned shop which was so useful then, but is rarely to be found in today's towns. The ladies in 1950s fashions walk past the railings of the Baptist Church. This would soon be rebuilt in modern form facing the Folly, transporting the original rose window glass.

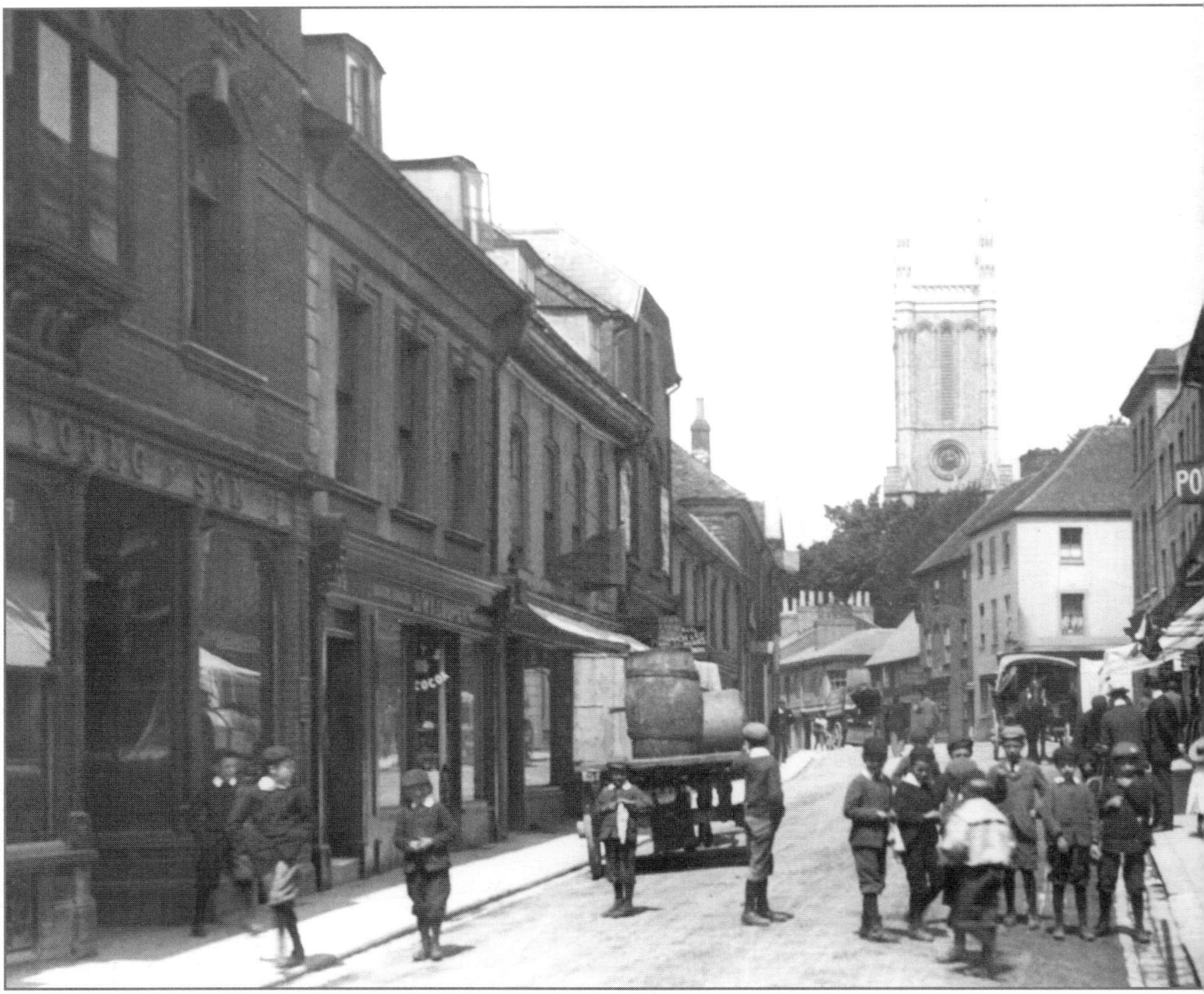

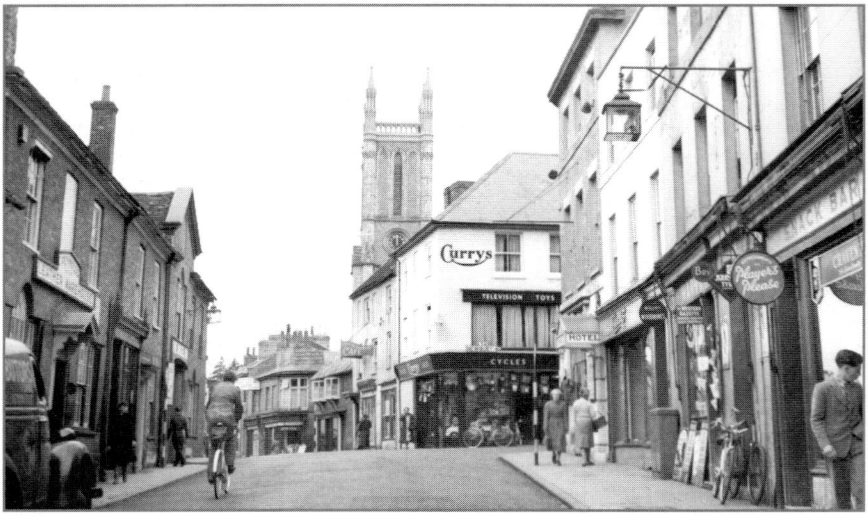

High Street c1950

A49031

The ground floor frontage and canopy below E Reynolds Leather Warehouse sign would soon be ripped out to make way for a hard-edged modern shop front. In the 1980s, a 'period' canopy would appear beyond with some degree of success. Harvey's newsagent and sweetshop (beneath the lamp on the right) has now changed hands.

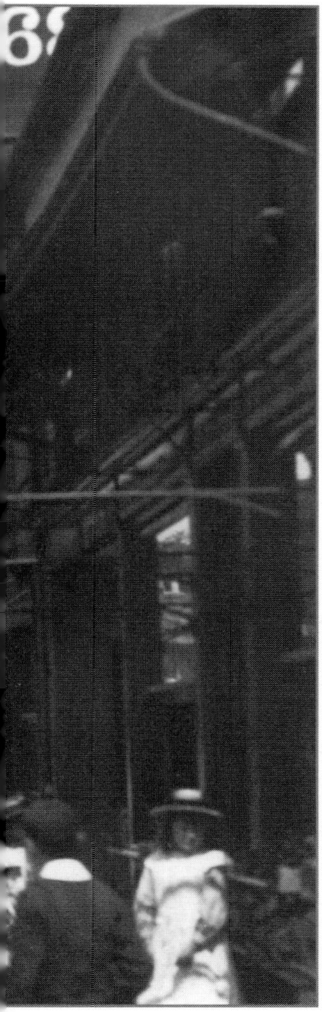

◄ **High Street 1901**
46346
With a bustle of children and hardly an adult in sight, it looks as if the Grammar School in New Street (before being remodelled as Church Close) was out for the day; there was little need in those days to watch out for traffic!

▼ **High Street c1955** A49055
It was from the window on the gable on the left, above the Angel's coaching arch, that magistrate Bethell Cox read the Riot Act to the mob of agricultural workers in November 1830, and was called a 'fat slug'. The rioters went to Anna Valley and wrecked Taskers machines, but stopped at midnight as the Sabbath hour struck. On Monday morning the Lancers from Winchester rushed out in force, ending the disorder.

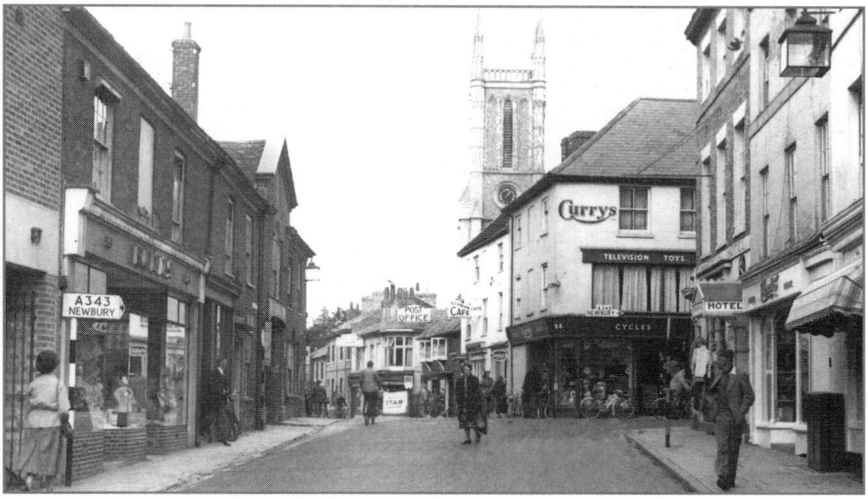

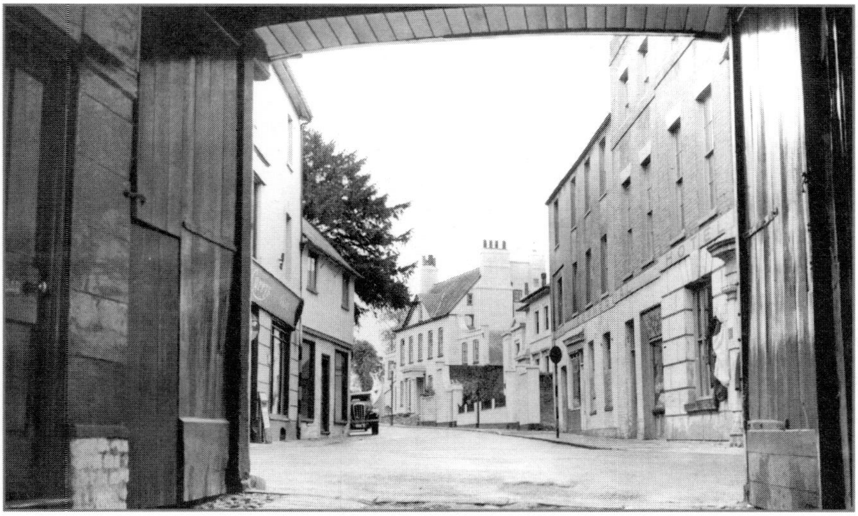

◄ **Newbury Street c1950**
A49048
The archway frames the old coach road from London. In 1435 fire consumed the town, leaving little but the Church and Priory. Across the road, the Angel's medieval College Inn was ashes. It was rebuilt ten years later on this side of the road. In its heyday, the Angel Inn's frontage stretched 30 metres north from the Chantry Centre's upper High Street entrance.

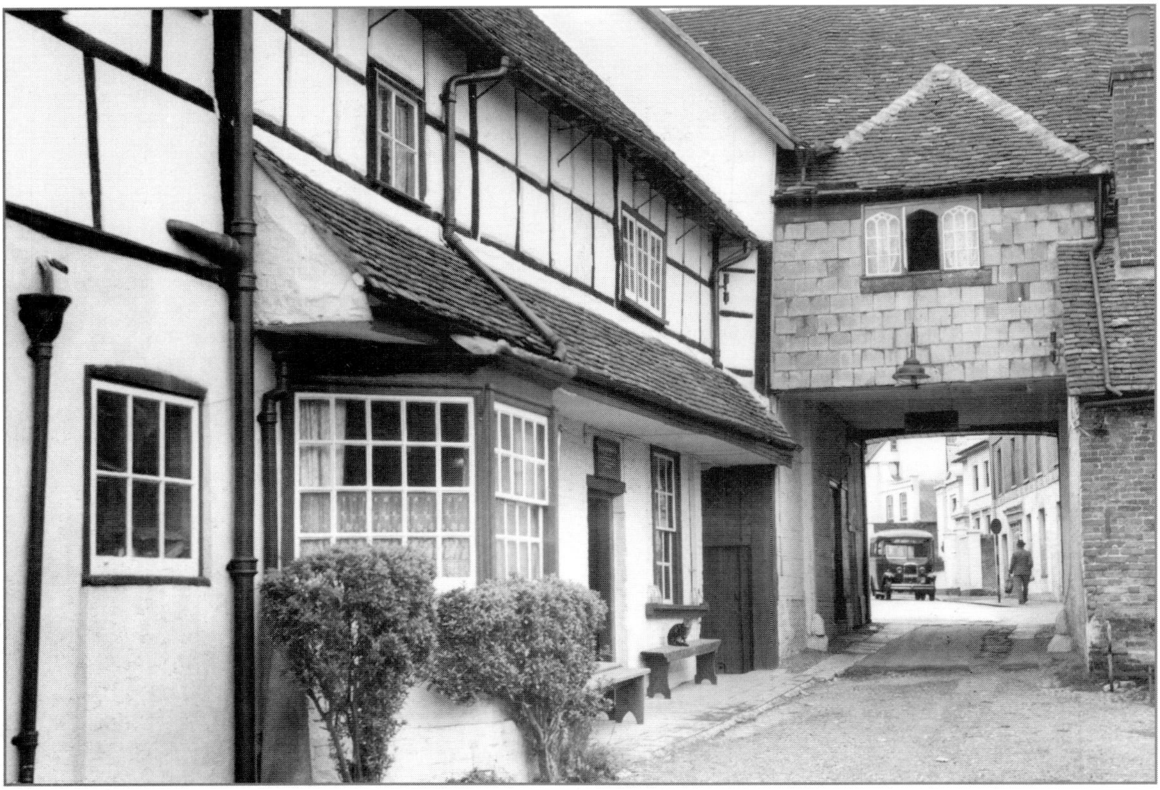

The Angel Inn c1950 A49047
Only parts of the north and east wings remain; the great range of stables has gone. Edward I, Edward II, Henry II, King John, Henry VI and Henry VII stayed here at the Angel, as well as Catherine of Aragon. James II dined here in 1688, failed to raise support and fled to London and exile. It is said that King John's door, saved from the fire, is still in the Angel and that the inn's ghost is a black dog!

Approaching Town by St Mary's Church

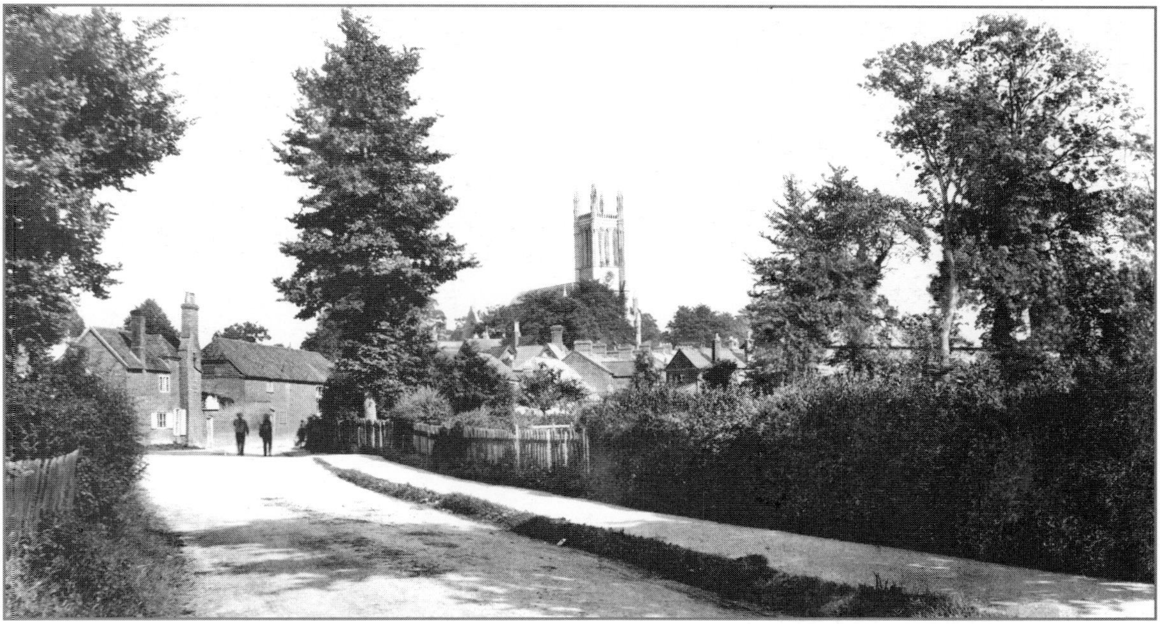

From the North West 1898 42079
The most scenic approach to the town is from the north. A century on, the view of Church Hill in Marlborough Street is still easily recognisable, despite the two great complexes built on each side of the road, the Lloyds TSB Training Centre on the left and Cricklade College on the right. The first building in the picture is the Anton Laundry; today by appointment to His Highness the Prince of Wales.

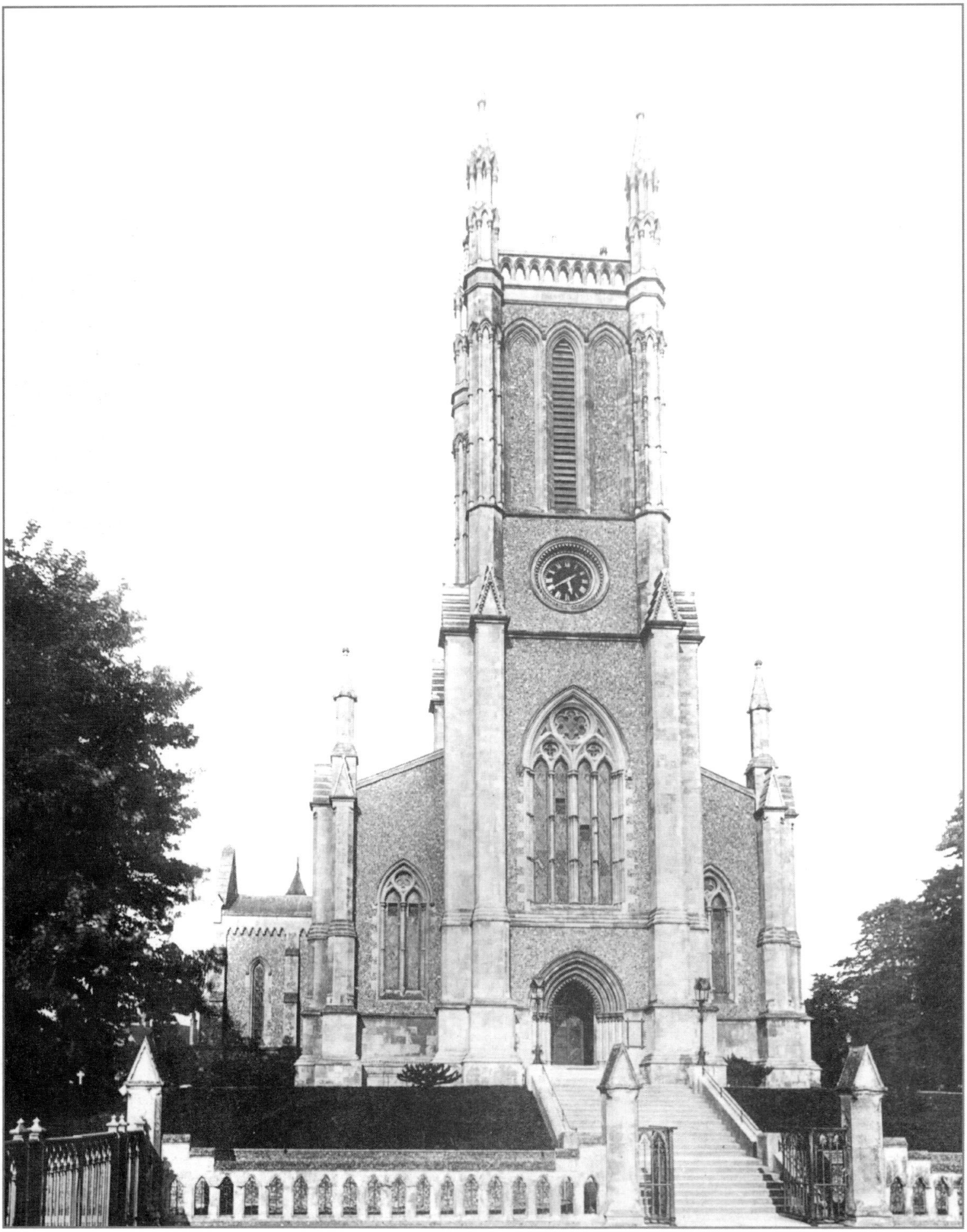

St Mary's Parish Church 1899 43690
The parish church stands majestic at the top of Church Hill, as it has done since 1846. Where the tree is seen on the left, St Mary's Church Centre now stands, sharing a forecourt with the modern flats of Gale Court.

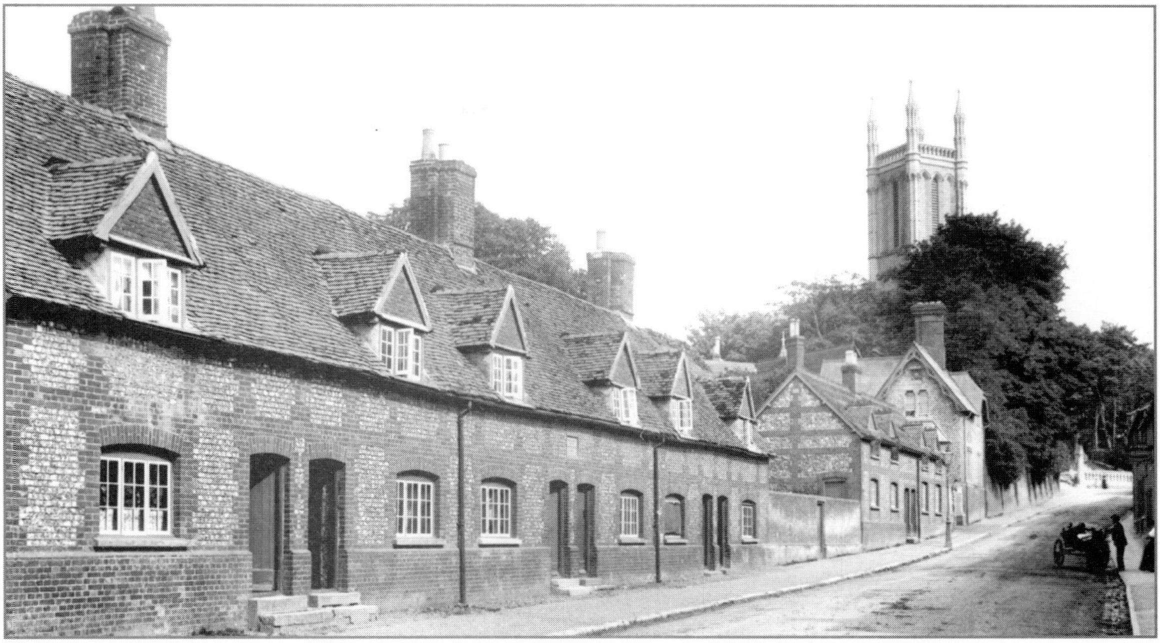

John Pollen's Almshouses, Church Hill 1904 52136
The block of six houses inscribed 'Erected by John Pollen Esq 1686' are all now privately owned. Gale Court would be built in the 1980s in memory of Martha Gale, replacing the trees beyond the houses. In medieval times, the road was Dog Pole Lane.

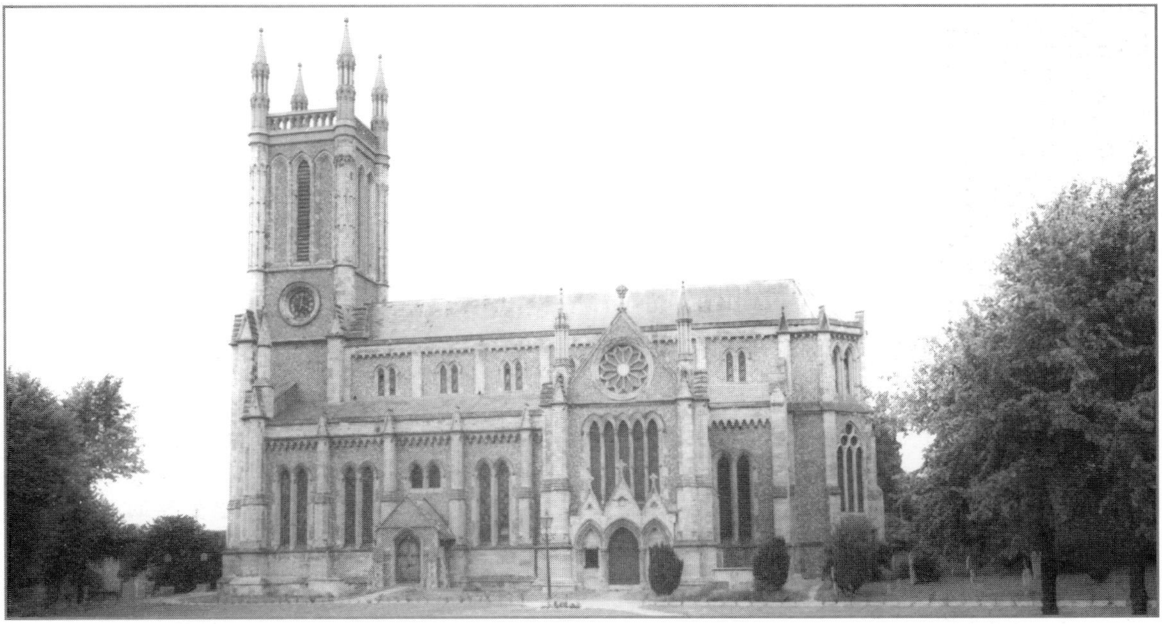

St Mary's Parish Church c1960 A49102
Architect Augustus F Livesay's design is a fine example of Early Victorian Gothic. The walls are of Caen stone and squared flints, the latter a mark of quality. Unfortunately, the stone was not all laid on its natural bed and so tends to spall badly. A workman was killed when some high-level walling collapsed during building. Sydney Smirke, brother of the architect for the British Museum, was employed during completion as an additional expert.

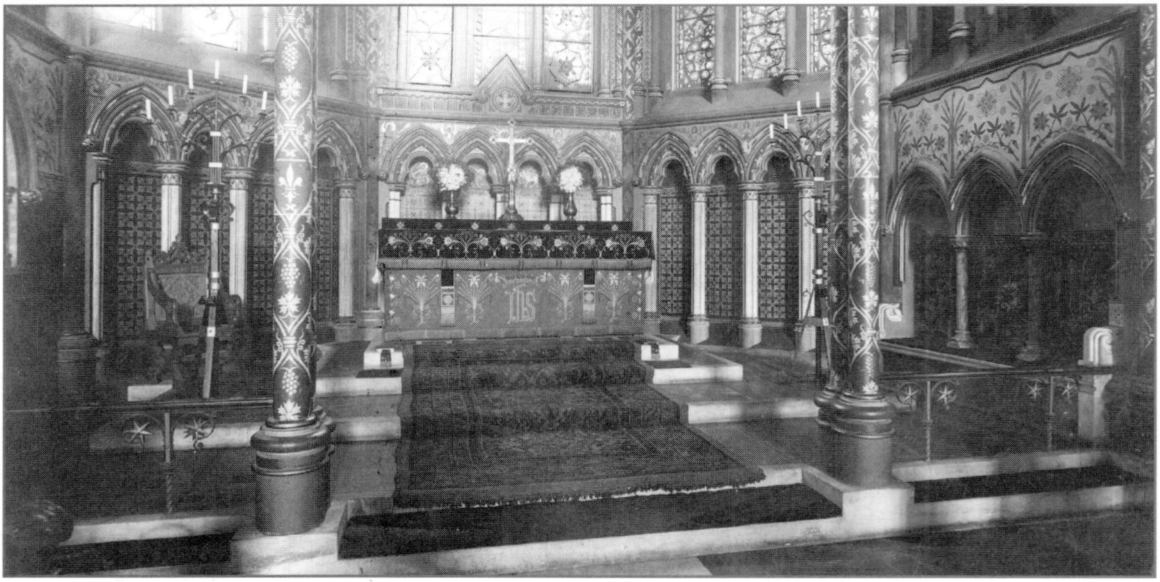

St Mary's Parish Church, The Chancel 1899 43691
St Mary's has been called 'the Cathedral of North Hampshire' and it is said that the arcaded walling around the sanctuary was inspired by Salisbury Cathedral. Only Tasker's cast-iron could make possible such slender columns on the chancel steps. Polychromatic wall decoration such as this evolved from around 1850, and became fashionable in the mid-Victorian period. The Rev. Philip Braithwaite, vicar of Andover, paid for E Geoffrey Grey to paint the chancel in a rich intricate pattern of red, green, gold and cream in time for the Easter Service in 1892.

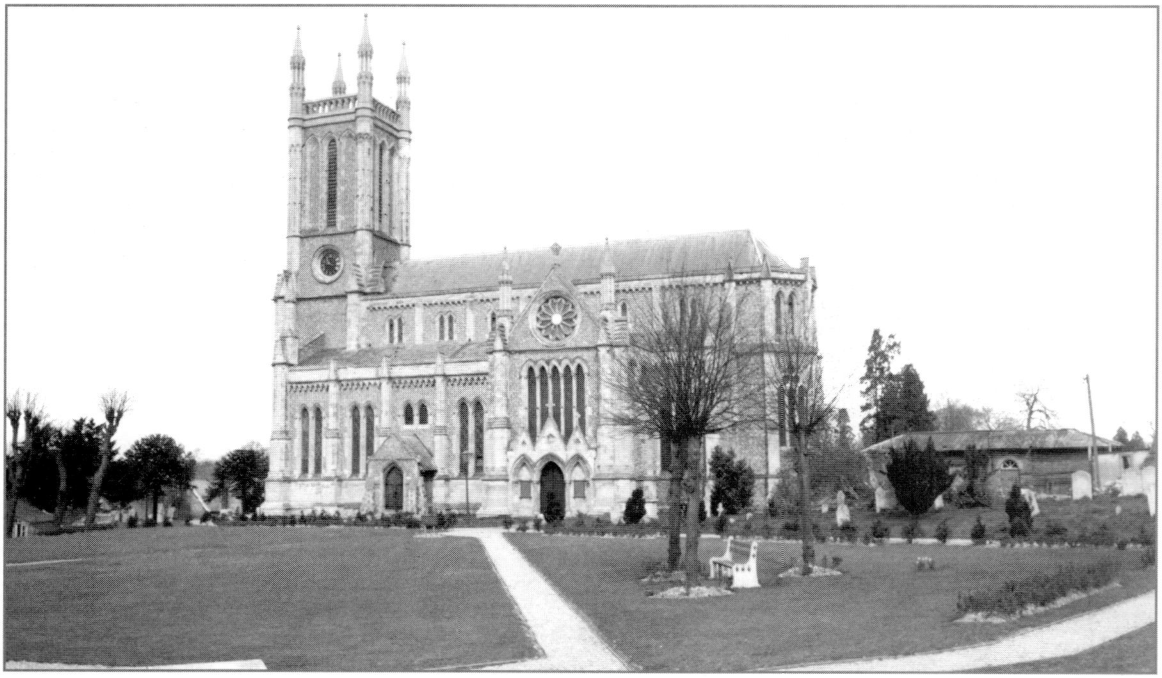

St Mary's Church c1960 A49075
Seen here from beside the War Memorial, shortly after the Garden of Remembrance had been created in 1947, St Mary's Church stands in sharp silhouette. Andover people can be justly proud of their church.

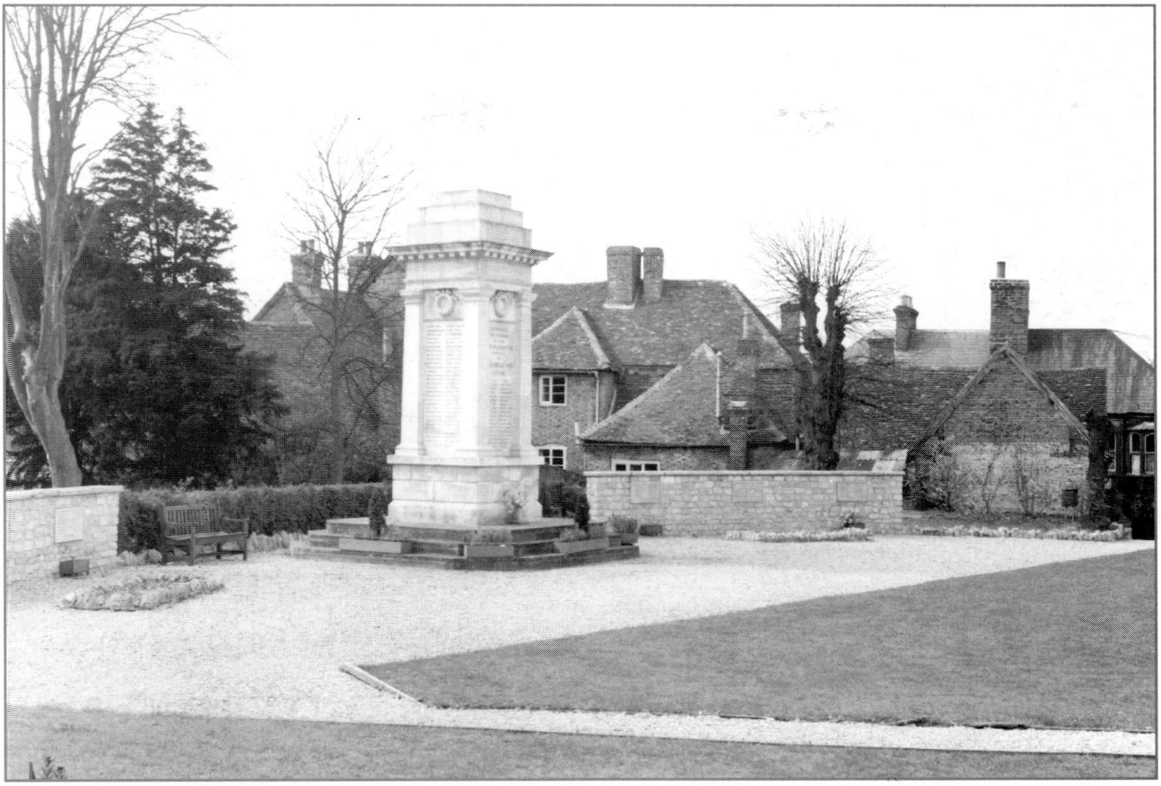

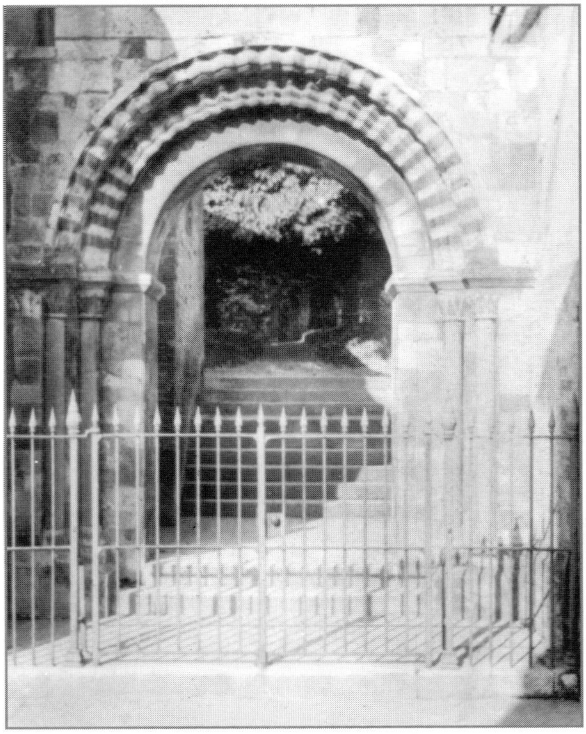

The War Memorial c1960 A49081
War memorials face the church across the Garden of Remembrance, a fitting place for six plaques on curved walling for World War II, 1939-45, and the Cenotaph for World War I, 1914-20. The unusual date accords to a battalion of the Hampshire Regiment that, sent to Archangel, remained in Russia fighting revolutionaries until 1920.

The Norman Gate 1889 43697
In the south-west corner of the Garden of Remembrance, the Norman Gate gives access from the High Street. The west door of the old Saxon/Norman church, it was moved to its present position in 1845 while the new church was being built. Here it is seen before the garden was cleared in 1947. The 1873 Ordnance Survey map showed a fire engine house, belonging to the Sun Insurance Company, behind the building on the right.

The Grammar School, New Street 1906 54623

In 1848, Dr Goddard's niece and heiress, Martha Gale, pledged money and gave the 1742 house on the left of the picture in return for having the school moved to clear her view of the church. A three-gabled classroom block was later built in 1888. The school went to Croye Close in 1925. Lord Denning, a famous former pupil, re-opened the Old Grammar School building as the Andover Museum in 1981. The Iron Age Museum followed in 1986. By this time New Street had been diverted behind the building and Church Close created.

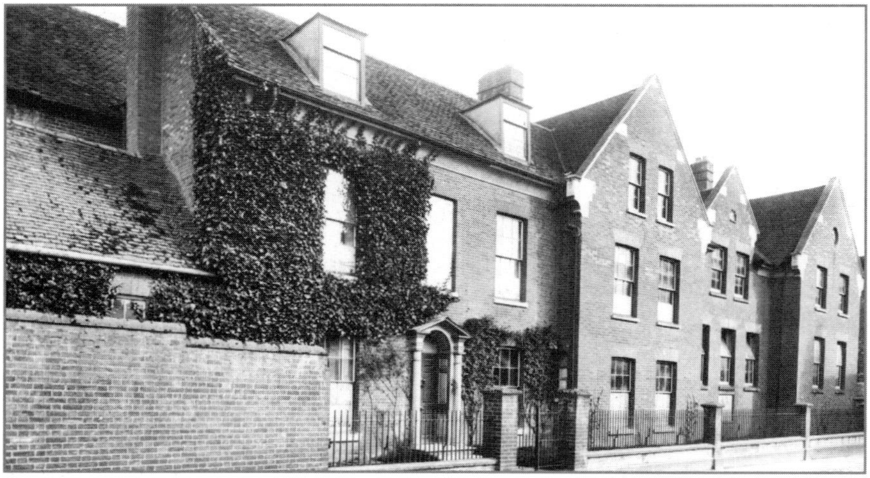

The Grammar School, Croye Close c1950 A49007

From 1925, Andover Grammar was relocated about a mile from Church Close, off Croye Close, and combined with a mixed school. In 1974 the new school became John Hanson Comprehensive School. Now in 2001 it is to move to a new building with extensive playing fields at Floral Way.

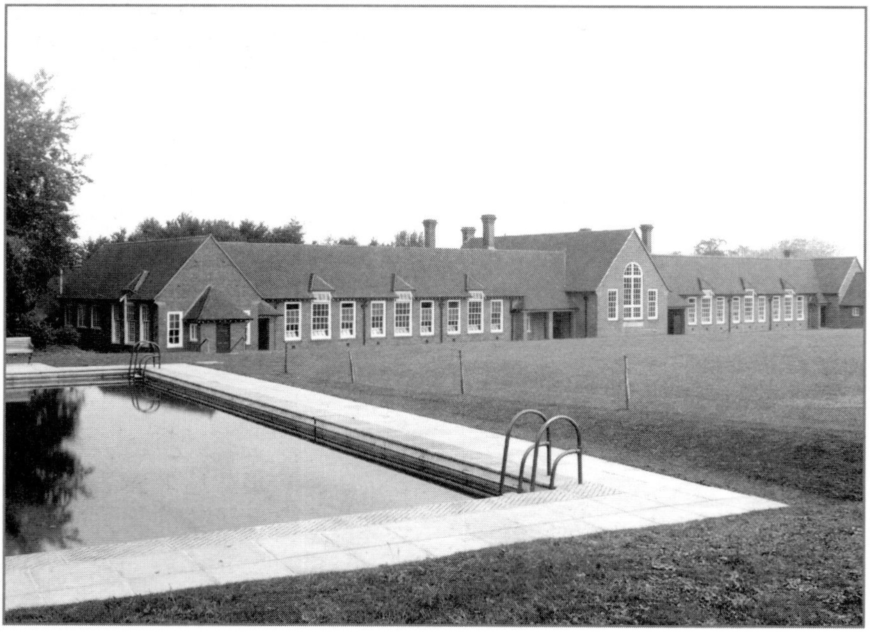

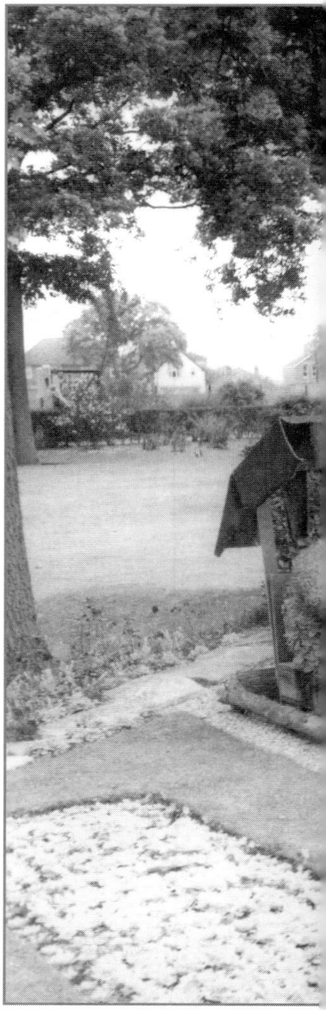

The Recreation Ground c1965 A49104

This quaint scene beside the aviary yielded to a new roundabout where Eastern Avenue/Newbury Road crosses the old coach road to London, New Street/Vigo Road. Birds still sing in the aviary, behind which a well-equipped children's playground has been installed. On the right, the narrow strip of park beyond the trees is the Common Acre, where the archers of Andover practised before going into battle under Henry V at Agincourt in 1415.

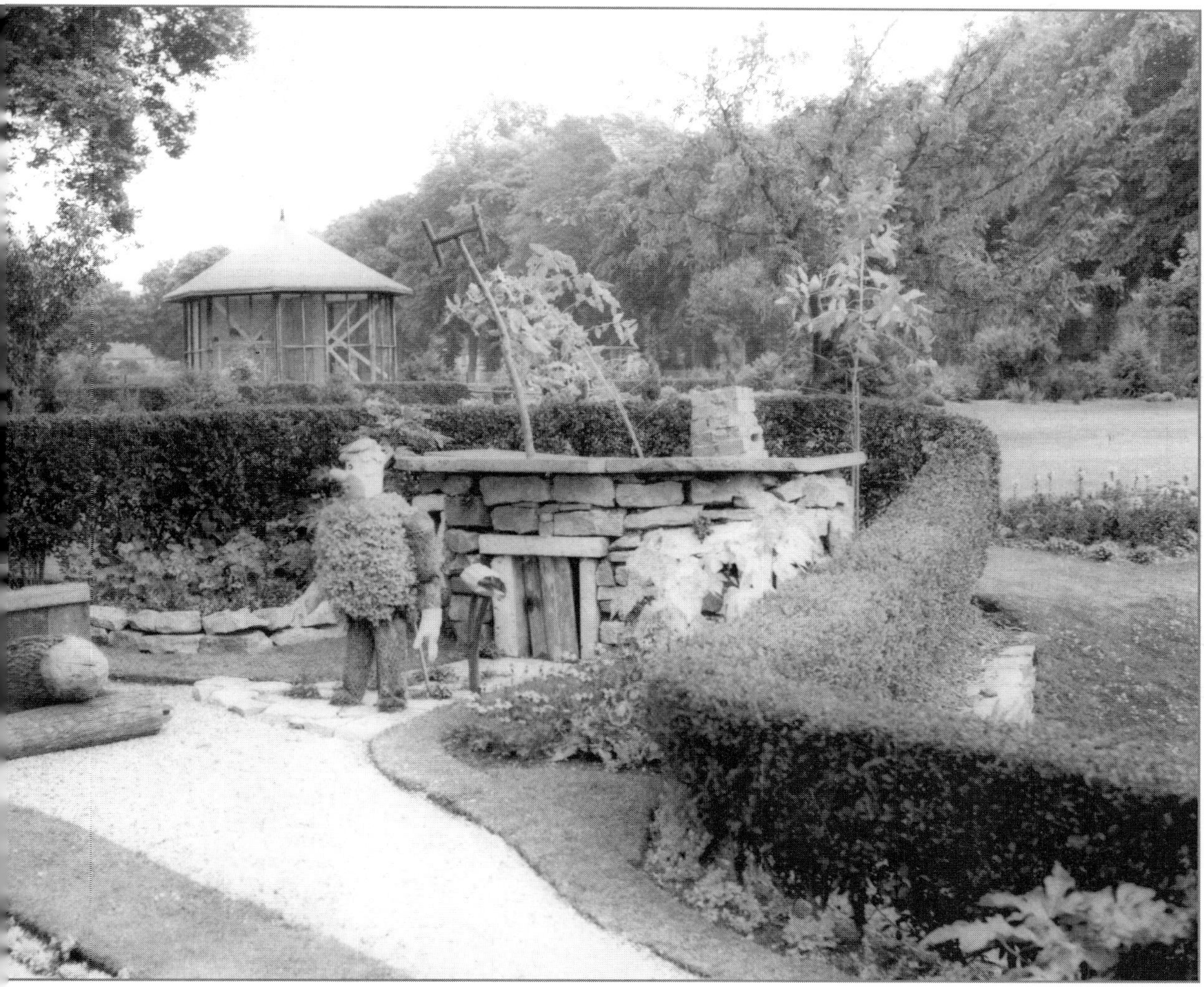

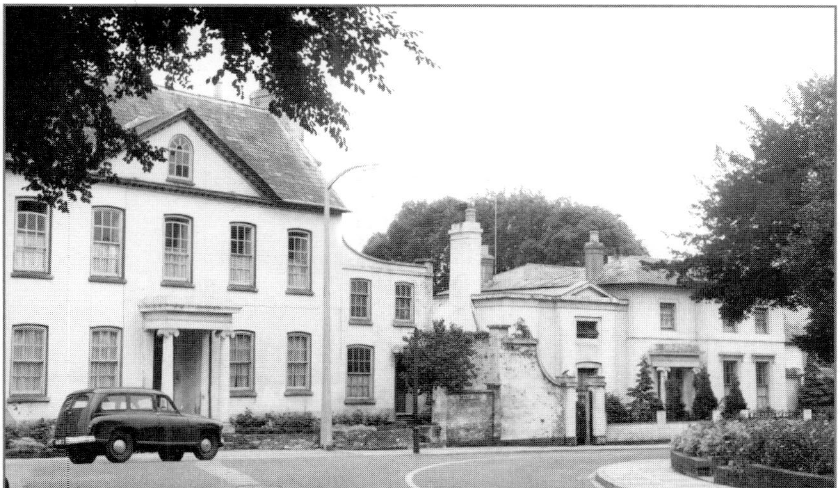

The Old Vicarage and Priory c1960 A49071
Dr William Stanley Goddard, headmaster of Winchester College, retired to Andover in 1809. In 1840 he engaged a young Portsmouth architect, Augustus F Livesay, and gave £20,000 for rebuilding the parish church. The first service was taken in 1844, but it was not until 1846 that the church was complete. In 1845 Goddard gave his fine Georgian house to the Church as a vicarage. Today it is occupied by a firm of solicitors.

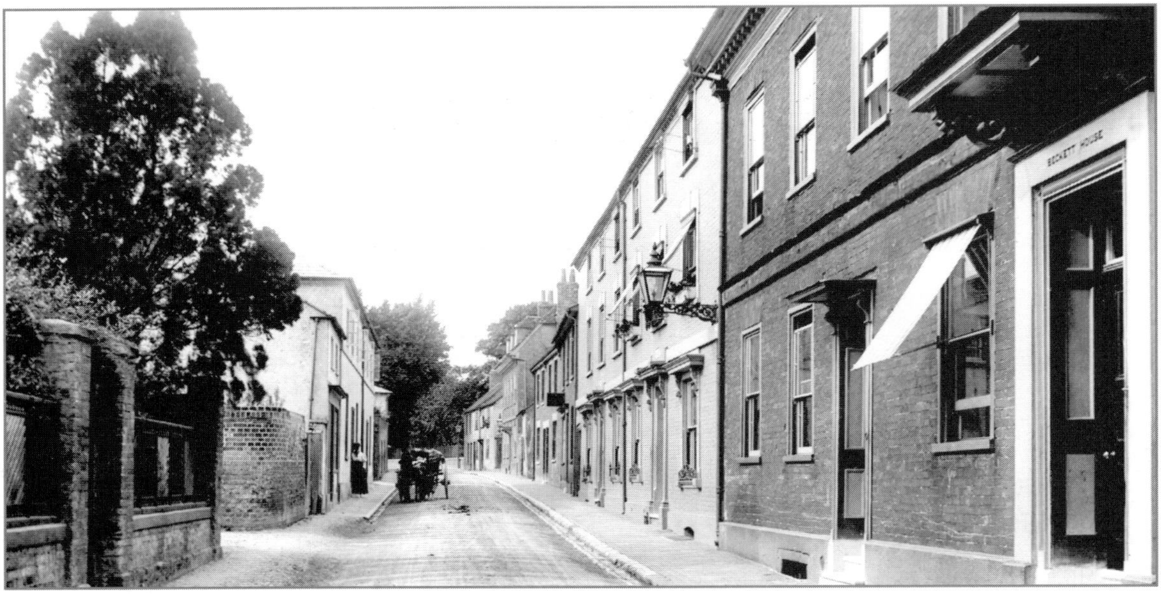

East Street 1904 52148
East Street used to lead from the Common Acre past a number of big houses. On the right, three dormers mark the roof of the Manse to the Congregational Church, built in 1780. In foreground right, Beckett House, now York House, retains its fine-jointed Georgian brickwork. Russell House, with the lamp, and Royston House are probably pre-Civil War, but were re-faced by Beales in 1887. The houses on the left were removed in the 1960s to make room for Eastern Avenue and Black Swan Yard car park.

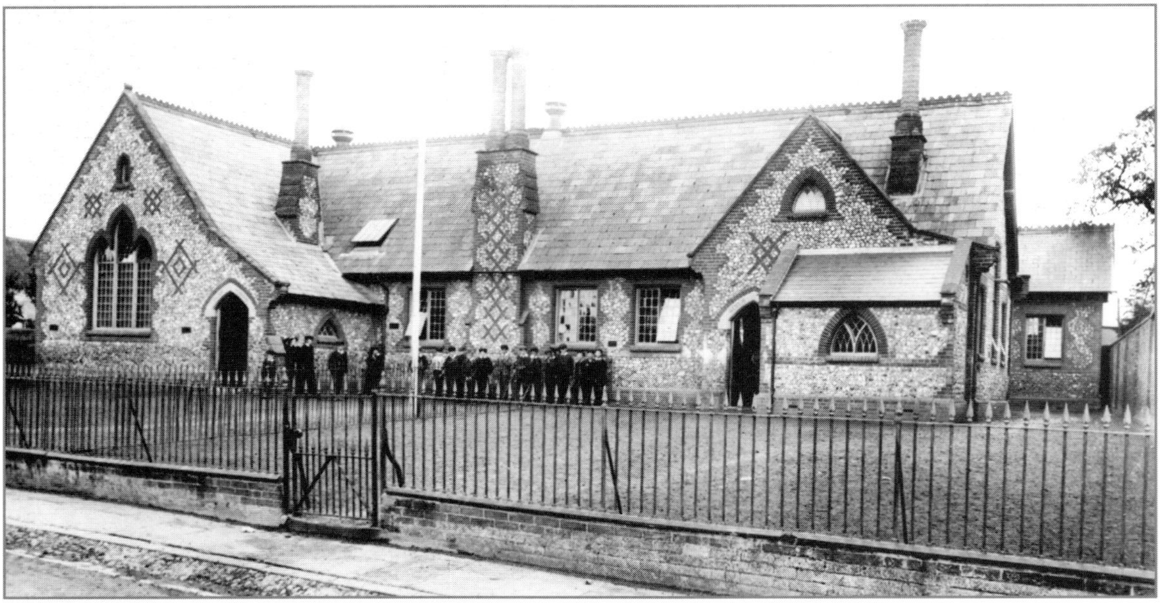

The British School, New Street 1906 54624
The British School of 1859, demolished in the late 1960s, was much like the National School, now Andover Primary School (C of E Controlled) which still thrives today in lower East Street. PLB Architects of Winchester extended East Street School in 2000 for Hampshire County Council, creating a pleasant polychromatic construction popularised by William Butterfield in the 1850s. The building is a fine example of its type, sympathetically adapted for today.

London Road and Exploring Ladies' Walk

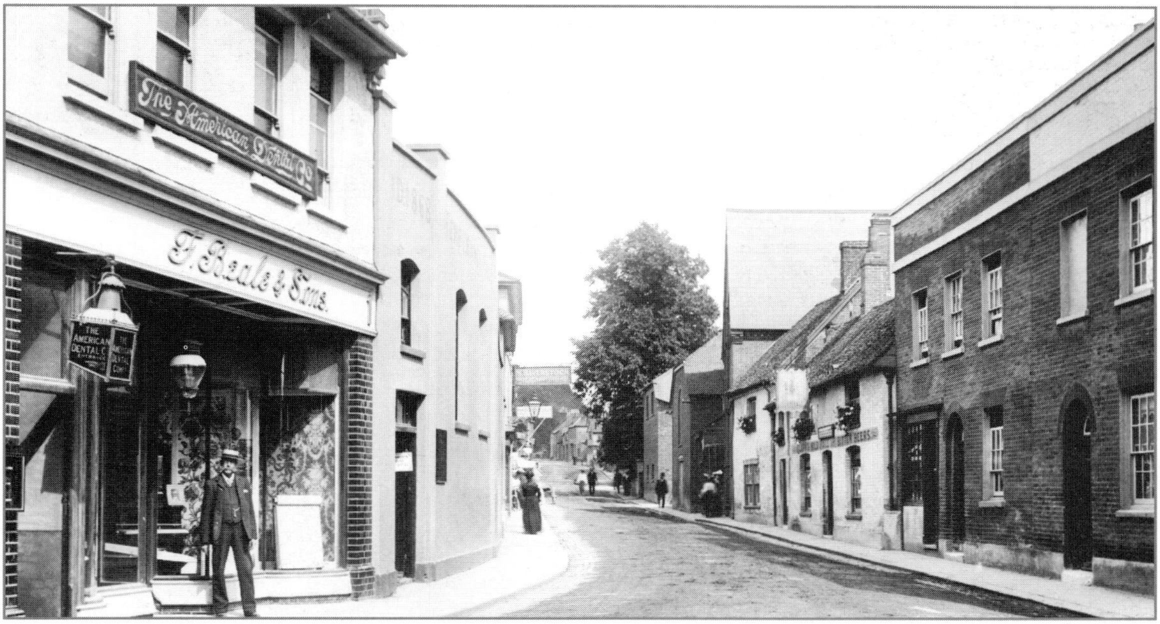

London Street 1904 52147
F Beale & Sons were builders until they were bought out in the 1960s. Their yard was in Adelaide Road, beside the swimming baths that they built in 1885. This could well be Frank Beale himself in front of their shop displaying carpets and wallpapers. The Temperance Hall of 1868 was next door, and across the road was the Forester's Arms, once a Heath family property, which still stands today.

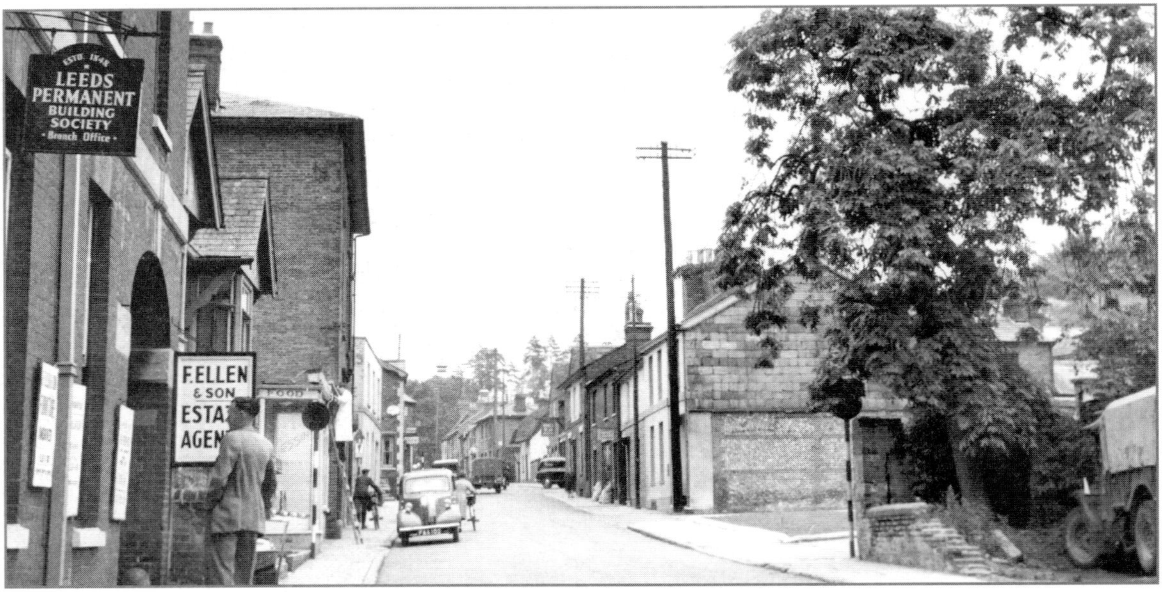

London Street c1950 A49027
Ellen & Son, estate agents, is where Gilbert & Heath opened Heath's Bank by 1807. Opposite was Heath's Brewery, started by Charles Heath in 1778, shortly before coaching reached its peak. Coaching sharply declined after 1845 when the railway reached the edge of town. An army vehicle is in the forecourt of today's Hogshead Pub, then Charles Heath's residence. Next door was William Hawkins Heath's house, which would be demolished in 1928 to make way for the Savoy cinema, desiged by Freddie Henshaw.

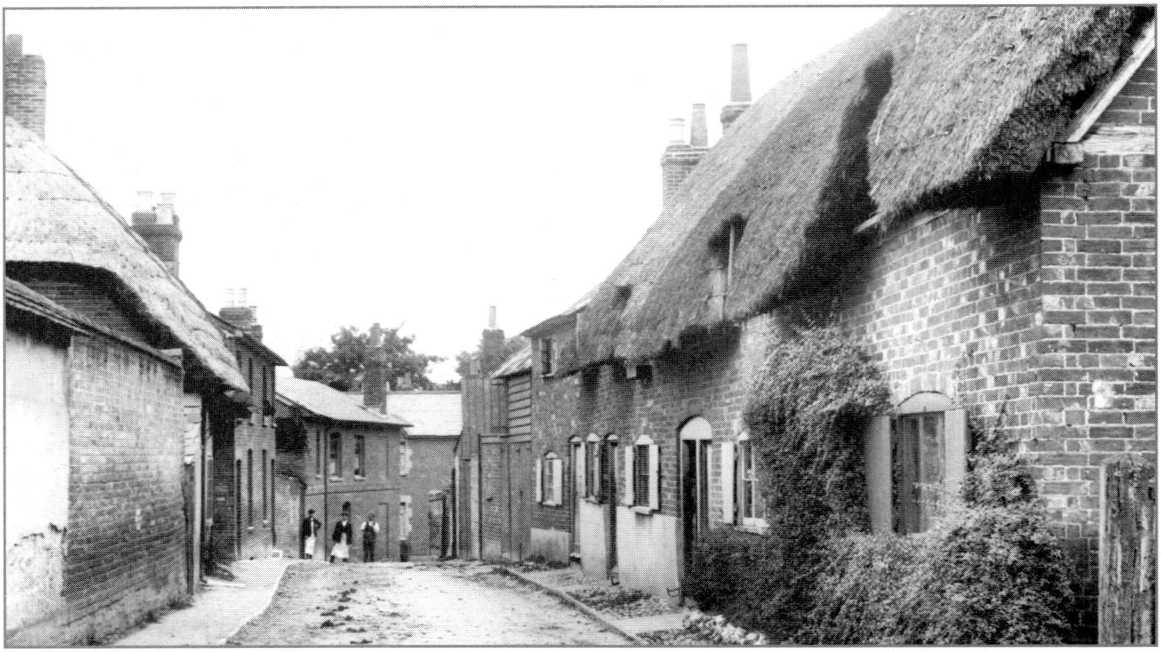

Dene Road 1904 52139
Off London Street, just before the King's Head, Dene Road is seen here dropping into London Street at the corner beside the King's Head. The thatched cottage on the left still stands. The thatch has long gone and the road is now kept clean.

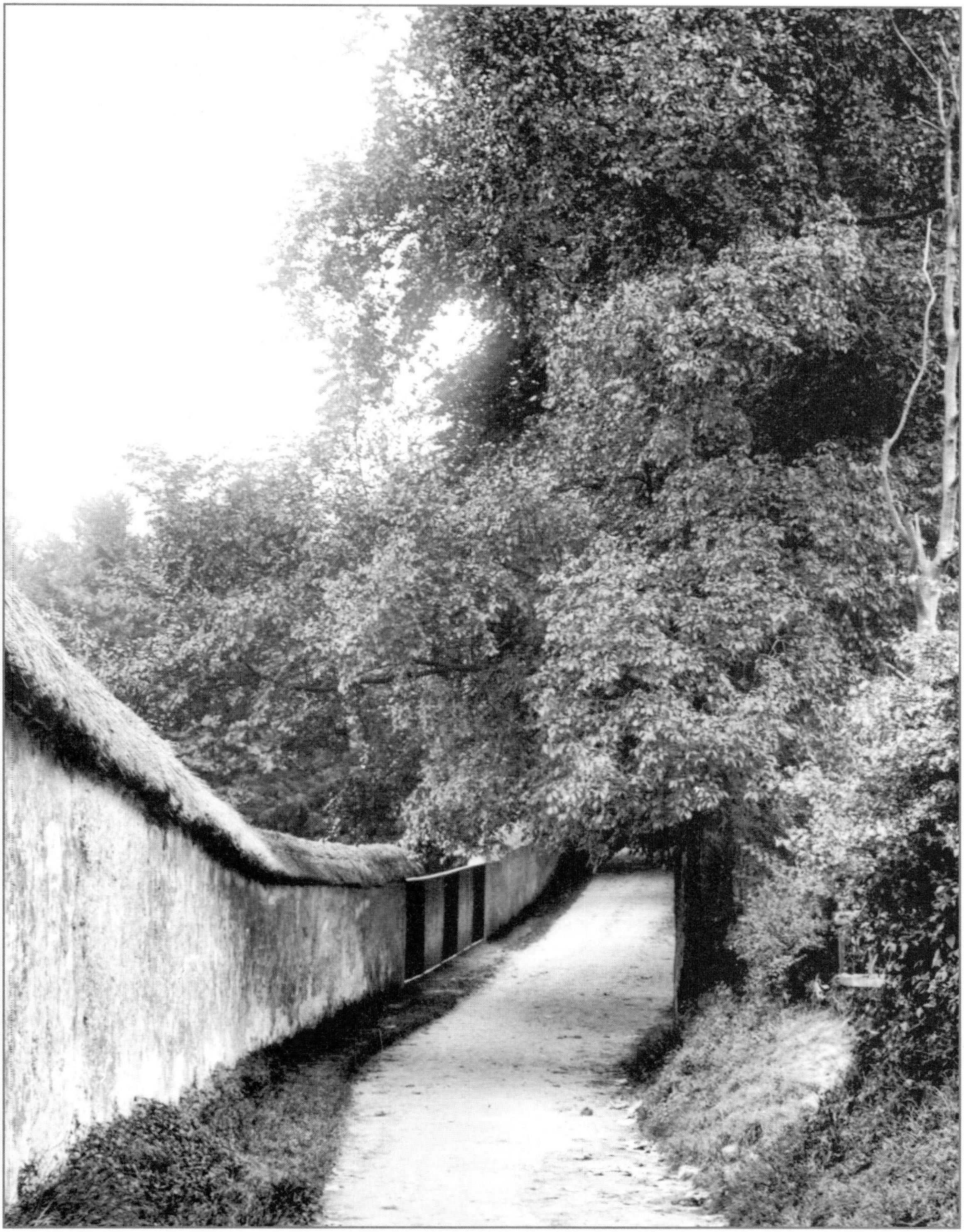

Love Lane 1904 52142
It is said that from time immemorial Love Lane was the place where ladies of questionable virtue would be found, and this is how it appeared a hundred years ago, just out of town.

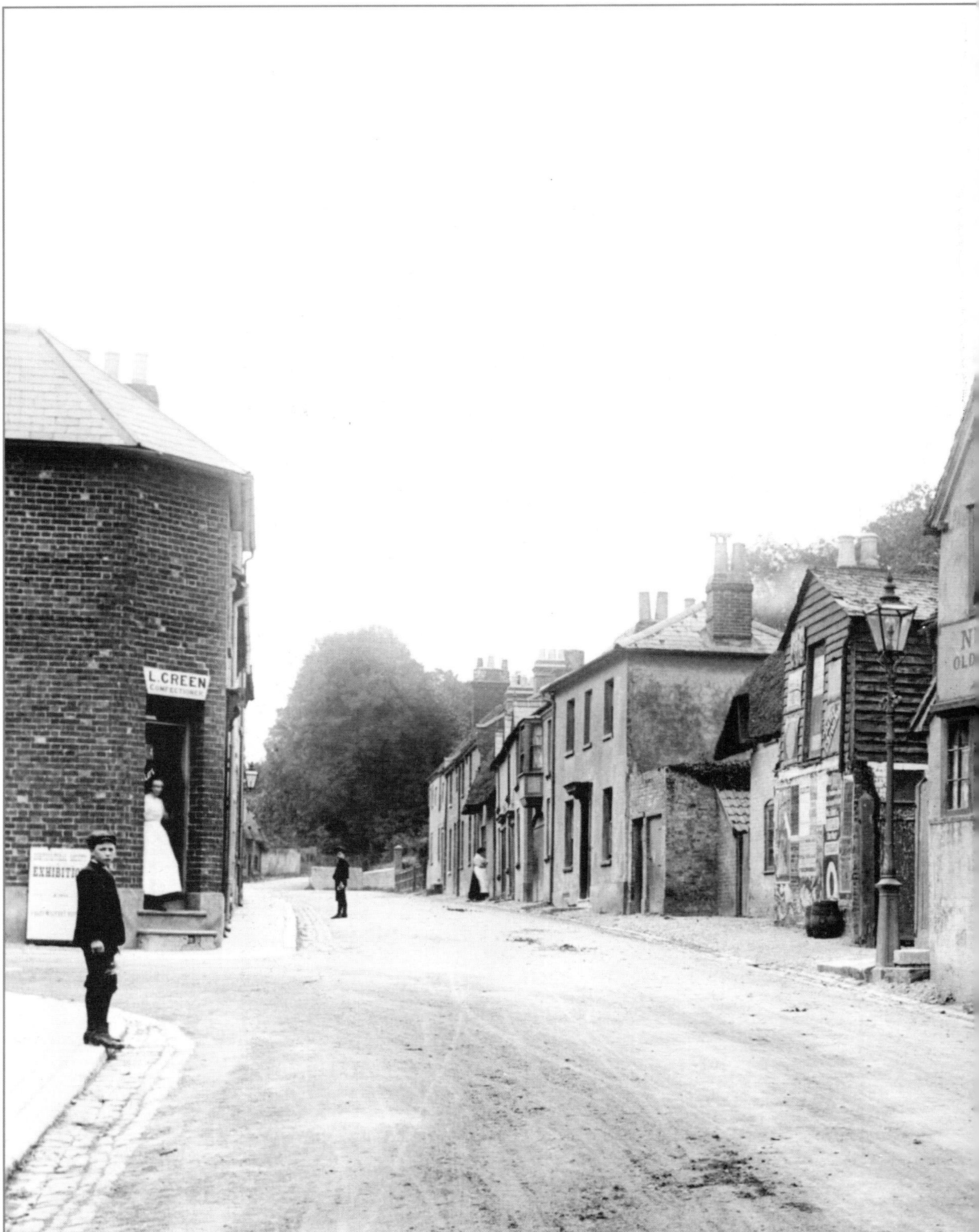
L. GREEN
CONFECTIONER
EXHIBITION

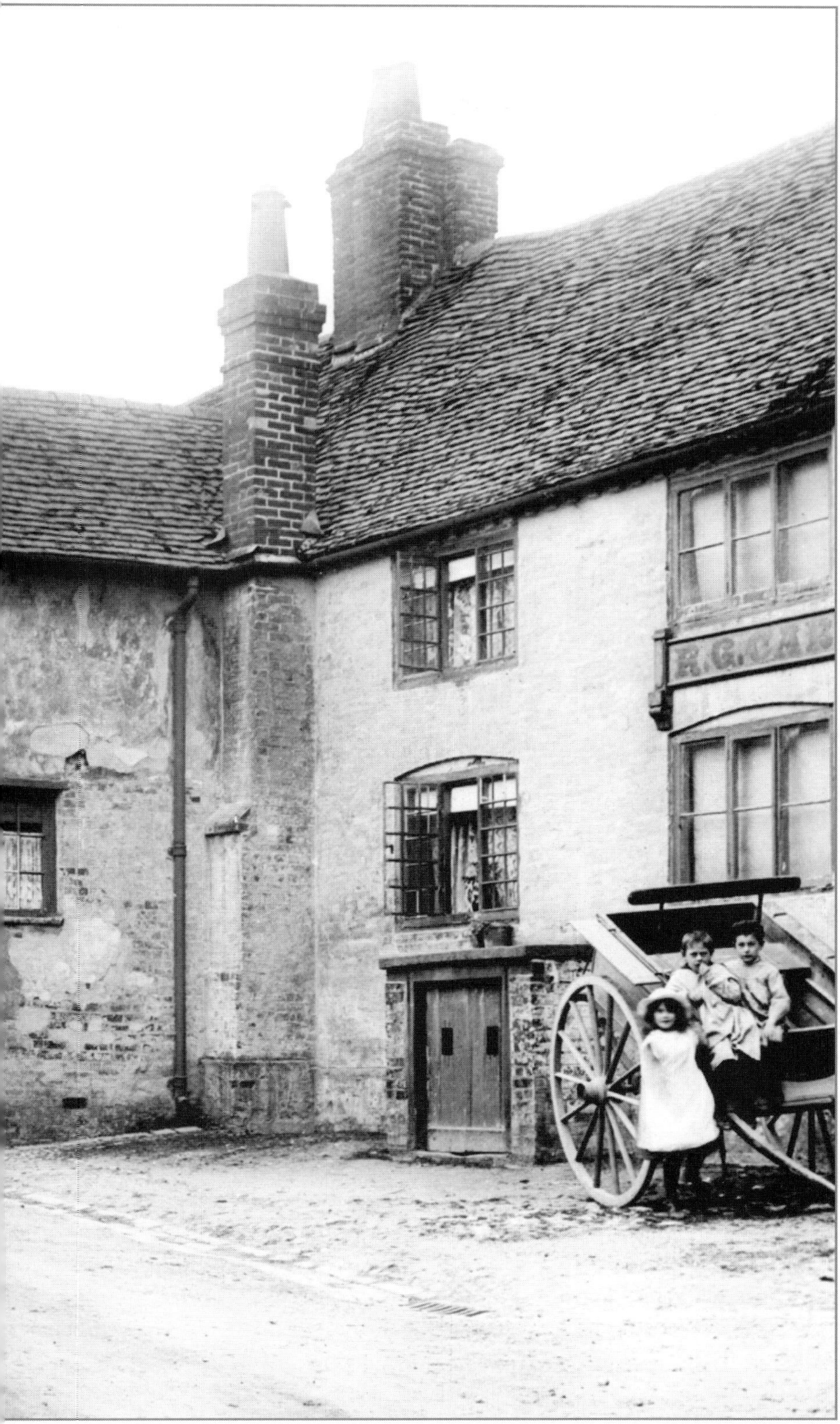

London Street 1904
52146
In the 1970s a corner shop would still be trading on the 1904 site of L Green's Confectionery Shop opposite Nutley's Alehouse, which, it was said, was only ever lit by candles. Nutley's was later rebuilt as the King's Head. In 1998 the licence would cease when the building became a shop selling drawing and office materials.

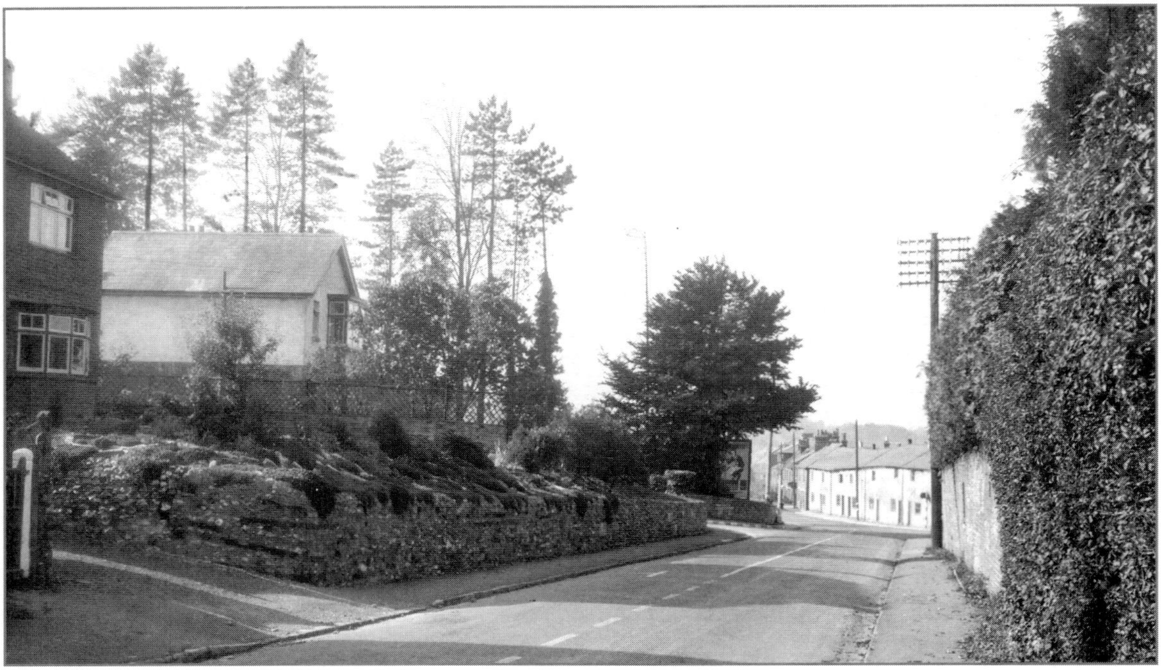

Micheldever Road c1950 A49009
Micheldever Road was a new turnpike in 1840 and would remain the main road from Winchester until town development after 1961 led to its abandonment. Half a mile behind the viewer is Ladies' Walk.

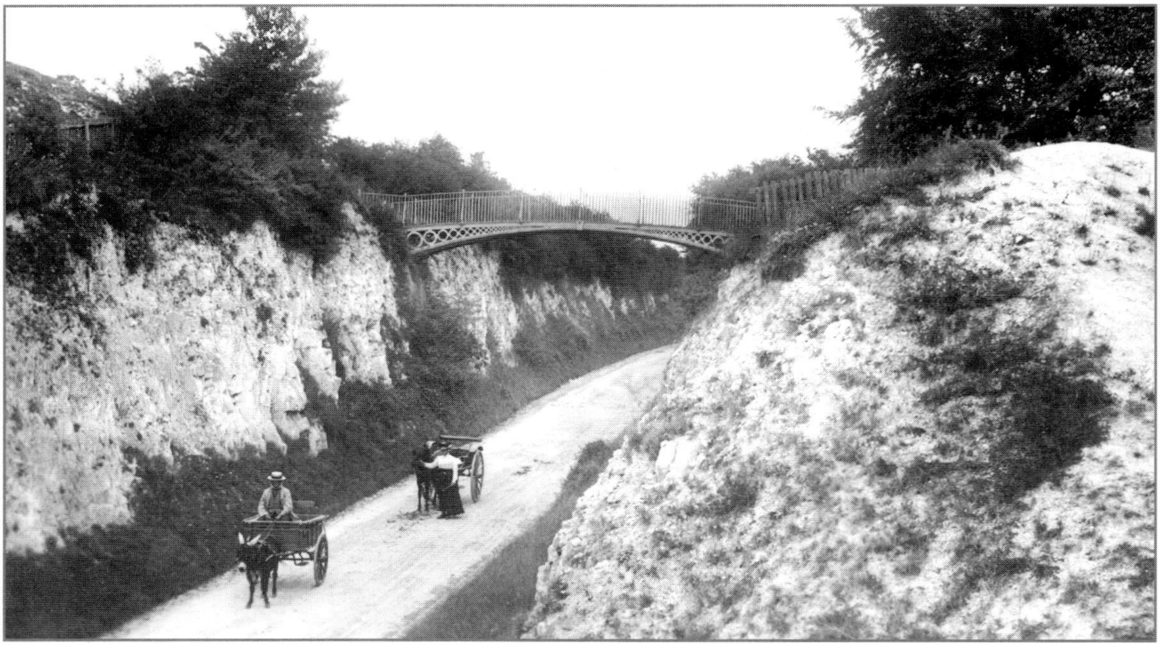

Ladies' Walk and the Iron Bridge 1904 52151
Just out of the picture, high on the right bank, is the path from Love Lane and Wolversdene Road to the bridge. The trap and donkey cart going into town have stopped to pose for the picture. Today they would be seen through a dense screen of bushes and trees.

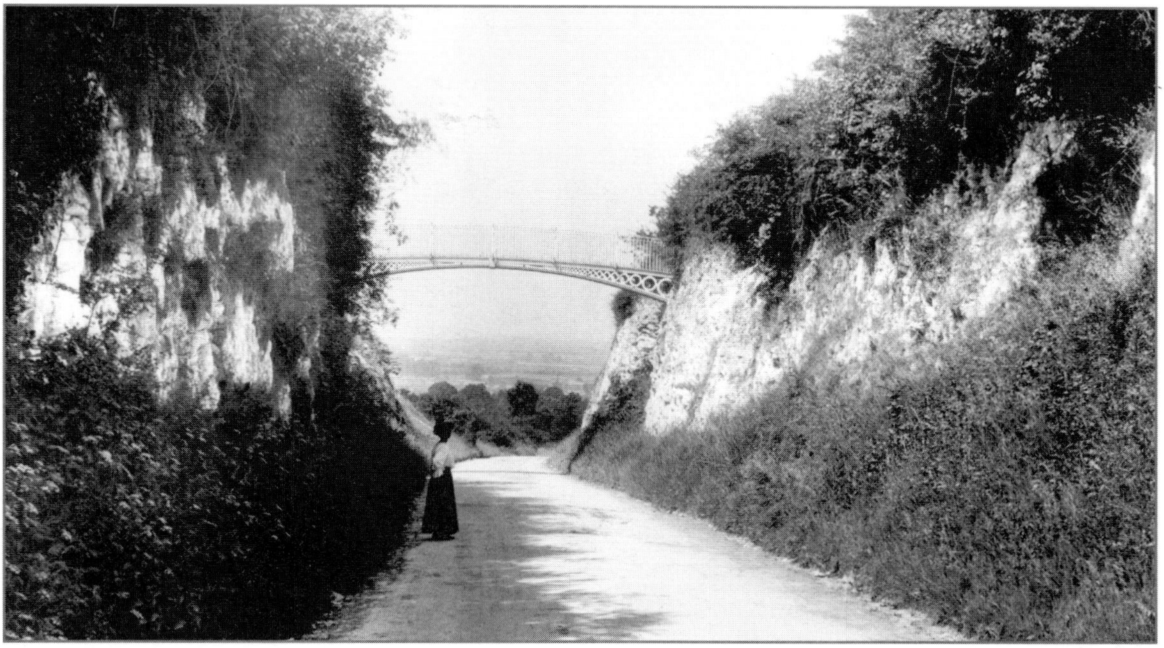

The Iron Bridge, Micheldever Road 1908 60098
In 1908, the view of the town looking back under the bridge was unobstructed. On the left, about 200 metres toward town, the path from Wolversdene Road crosses the access to the Quality Hotel and runs through the trees on top of the bank to the old Iron Bridge.

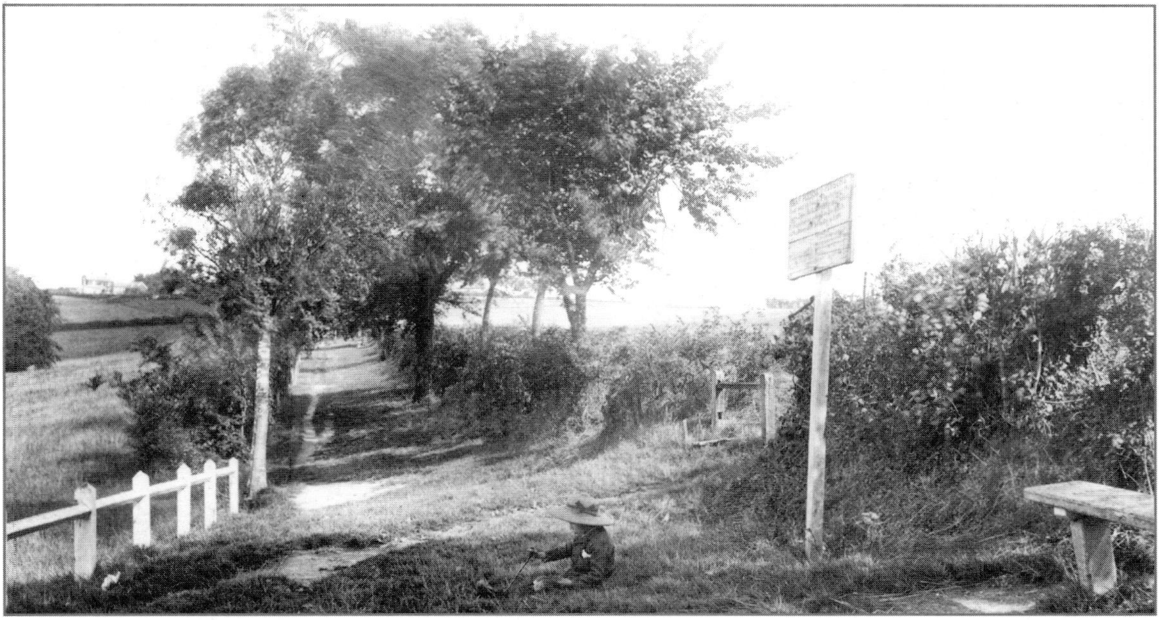

Ladies' Walk 1906 54629
On Ladies' Walk, across the bridge and about 100 metres east is a fine open view to the left over Highlands Road with Walworth Industrial Estate in the distance. In 1863, 121 trees were planted along the walk to commemorate the wedding of the Prince of Wales to Princess Alexandra. In 2001 heavy undergrowth was cleared. The trees have grown immensely but this view point is still there.

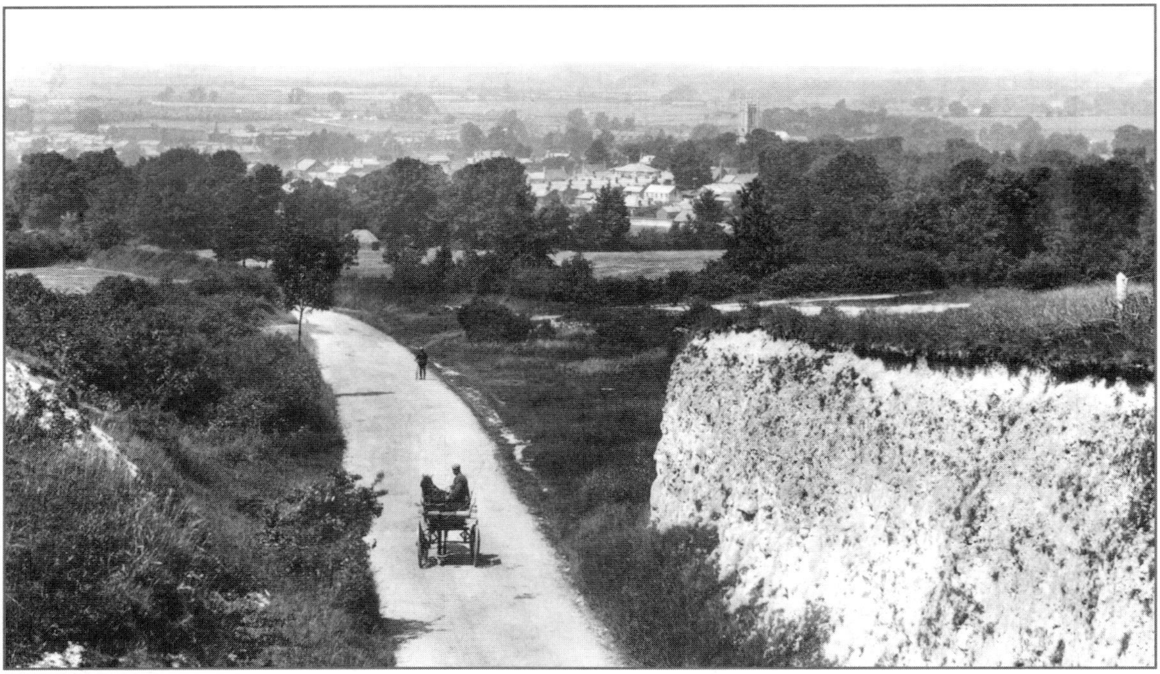

View from The Iron Bridge 1908 60099
Returning to the west end of the bridge, a most dramatic view of Andover was to be seen over Micheldever Road in 1908. Today, raw chalk has been conquered by soft greenery, obscuring the town.

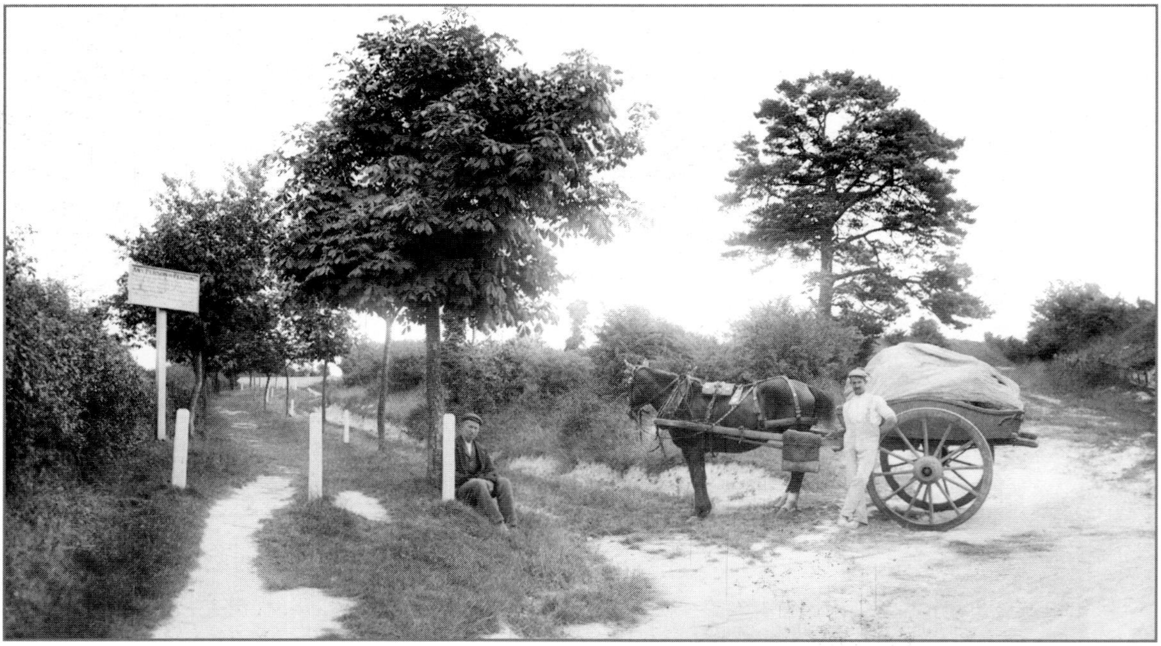

Ladies' Walk 1904 52150
Ladies' Walk ends a little more than a kilometre south-west of the bridge where the workman sits on Ladies' Walk. The road behind the cart leads to Bere Hill Farm. Old Winton Road, running behind from left to right, is the old Roman Road over Bere Hill to Wherwell and Winchester.

Ladies' Walk to Winchester Street and Town

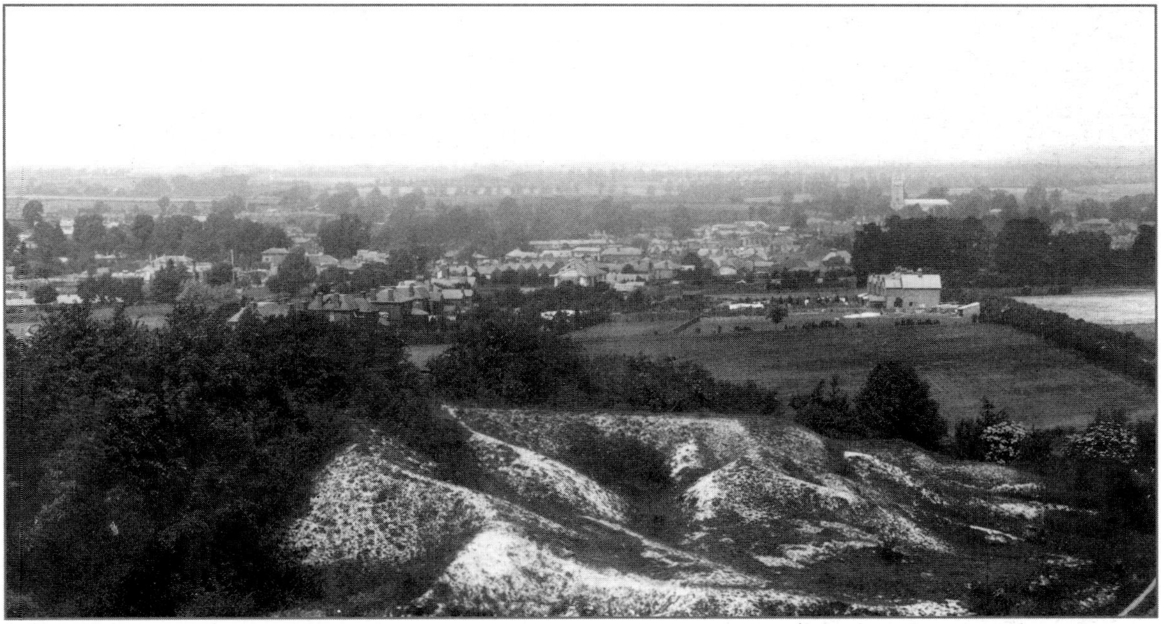

General View 1899 43689
This panorama takes in the Old Winton Road, which crosses on the right. A lone block of four houses were the only dwellings on that straight length of road in 1899. By 1905 a spurt of building would fill in the right-hand side all of the way into town. Later, the golf course would be constructed beyond the base of the mounds, and house building in this road would be virtually continuous on both sides by the end of the 1930s.

▼ **Winchester Street 1904** 52144

In 1904, Winchester Street became Winchester Road, where houses ceased and countryside began. Here the picture was taken with Old Winton Road behind on the right. Mr Wheeler on the left recovered umbrellas and chairs and repaired them. Except for the Lamb Inn, none of these buildings remained after the 1970s.

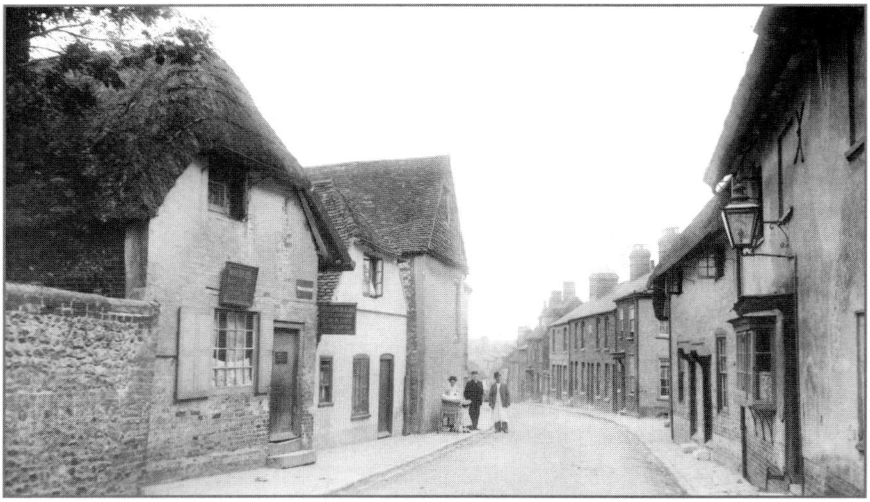

▼ **The Wesleyan Chapel 1904** 52138

The Methodist Sunday School's gable and simple rose window, built with the Church in 1824 in what was then Brick Kiln Street, were removed when the Salvation Army acquired the building in 1906 as their Citadel. Only the distant building with roof dormers, the Citadel, the house and the Lamb Inn on the right now remain. The Mason's Arms, two doors beyond the Lamb, was demolished with all the rest in the 1970s.

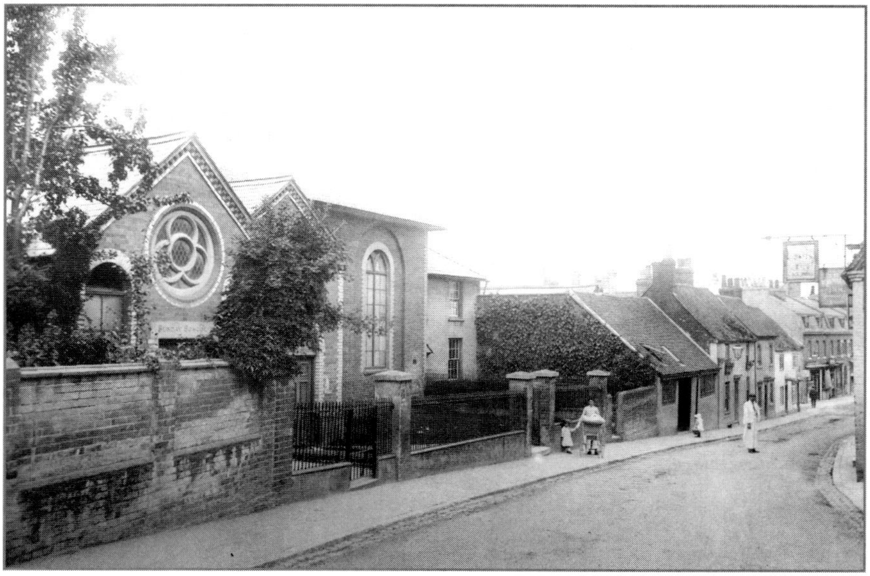

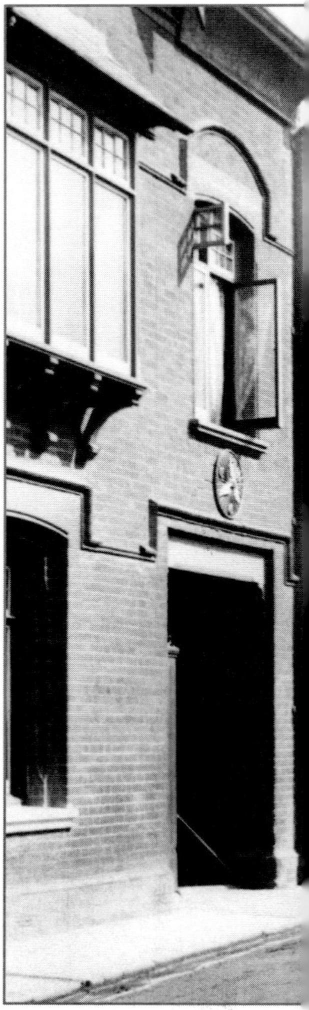

▲ **Winchester Street 1904** 52143

Morris's building, on the left, has boldly rounded eaves closers and moulded brick strings of better quality Victorian work. The design of the ground floor now suffers sadly from the modern shop fronts. The insubstantial building next door lasted well into the 1980s, when the best fish suppers in town came from the Fresh Fry therein.

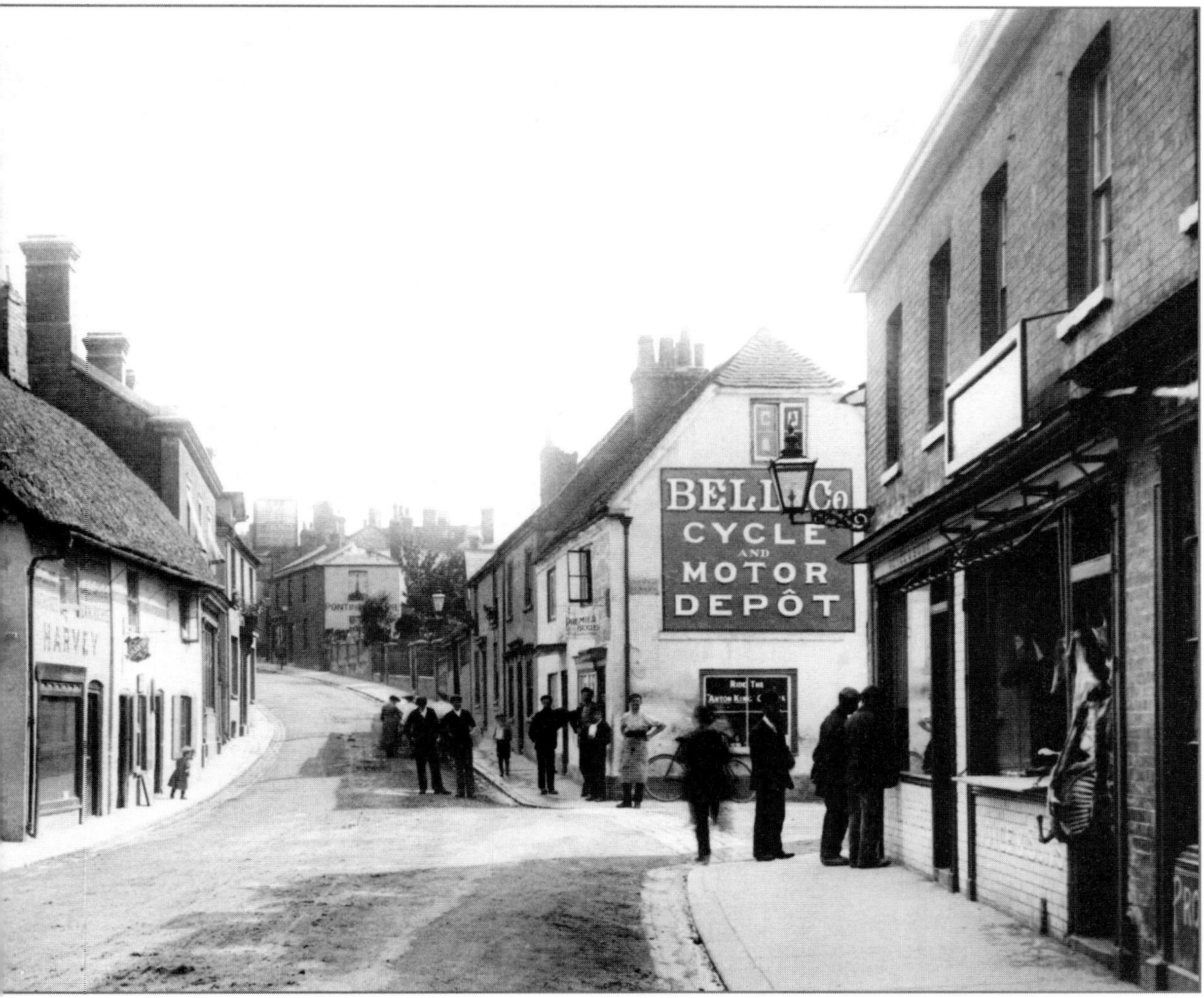

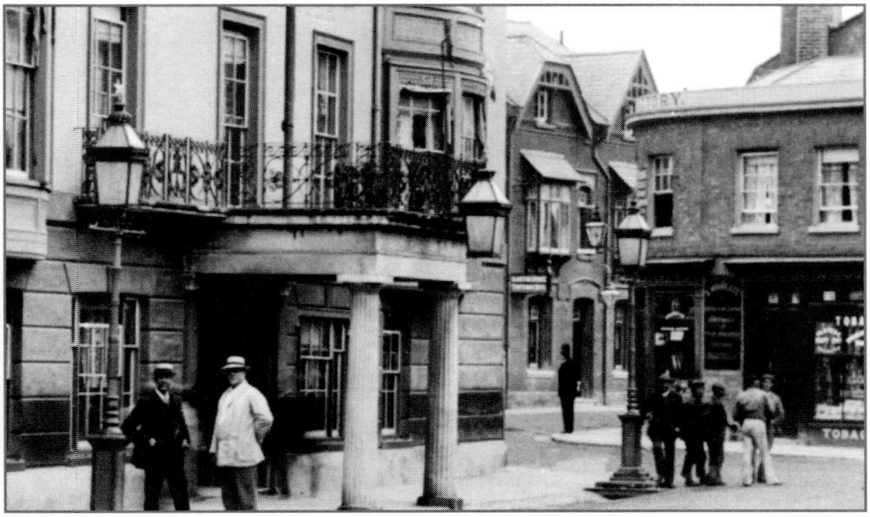

◄ **High Street 1904** 52149
Leaving Winchester Street and looking back at Morris's building behind the policeman, this was designed as Barton's Hotel by the architect for A B Scott's shop. The old brick frontage and entrance sat well under the twin gables, one clipped and one pointed.

Amport, Monxton and Abbotts Ann Villages

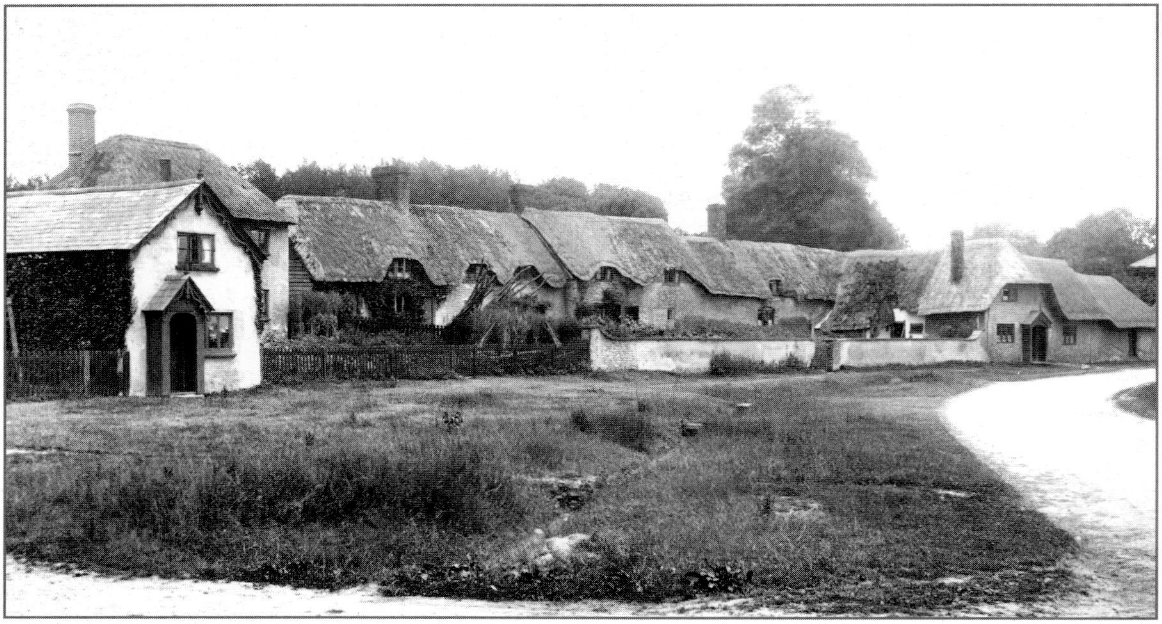

Amport, Cottages on the Green 1898 42092
The gardens and cottages of this rural set piece of thatch and village green today are neat and tidy. Off Church Lane to the right is Amport House, built in 1857, now the Forces Chaplains College, with Lutyens terraces planted by Jekyll. St Mary's Church in Church Lane is thought to go back to the early 16th century. A leading critic has written of the 'conscientious, tactful restoration, 1866-7, of an almost unique decorated church'. It is well worth a visit.

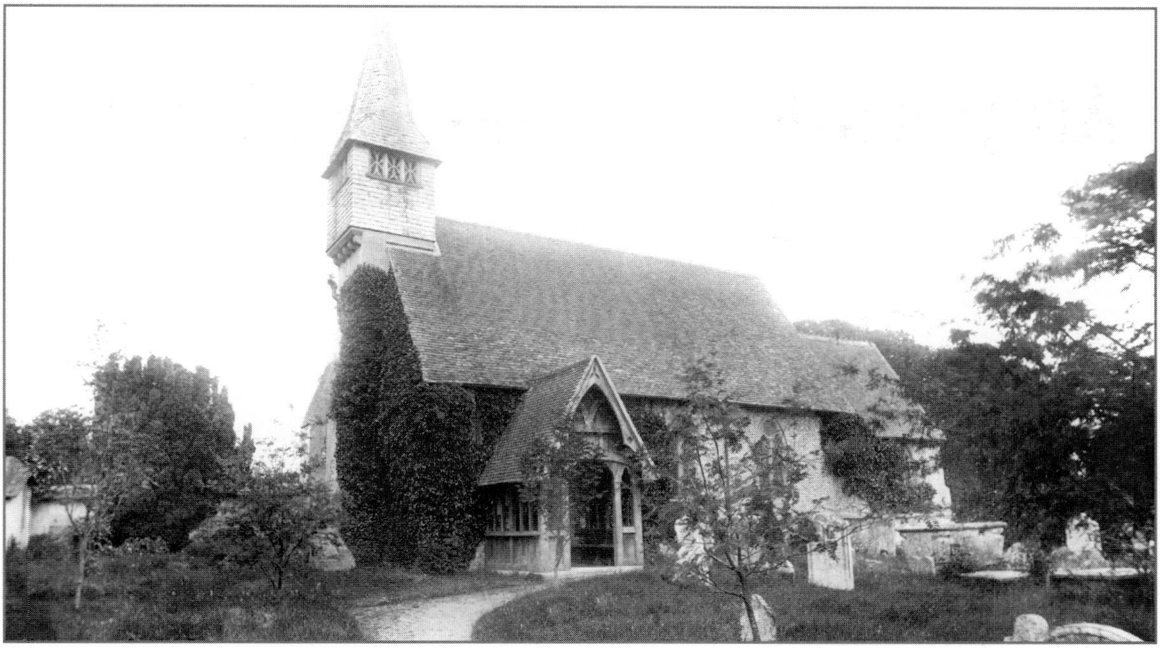

Monxton, St Mary's Church 1888 42090
Tucked away among trees by Pill Hill Brook, Monxton Church, with its shingle-faced belfry and broach spire perched on the gable, was rebuilt in early Victorian times. It typifies the many small churches to be found in the Hampshire villages.

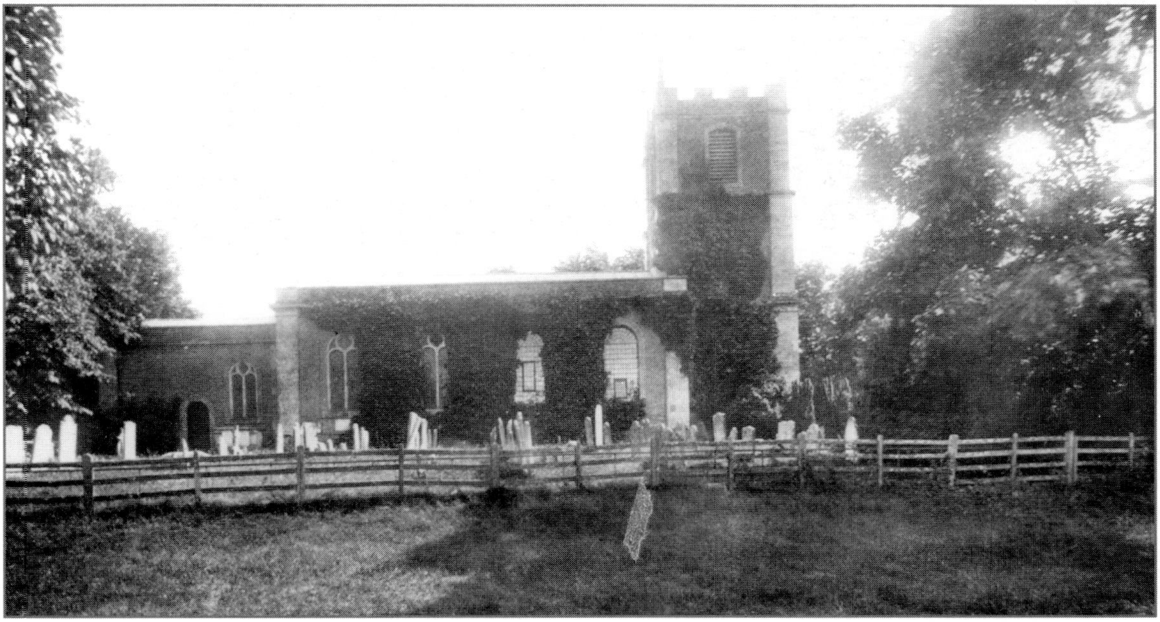

Abbotts Ann, St Mary's Church 1899 43696
Most village churches near Andover are older, altered or rebuilt Victorian. St Mary's, rebuilt in 1714, is a larger Georgian exception, seating 170 in box pews and gallery. The chandelier came from Andover's St Mary's when that church was rebuilt from 1842. The Georgian font is from another church. Hanging inside are paper Virgins' Crowns, each marking a past village spinster or bachelor - the most recent was put up in 1973.

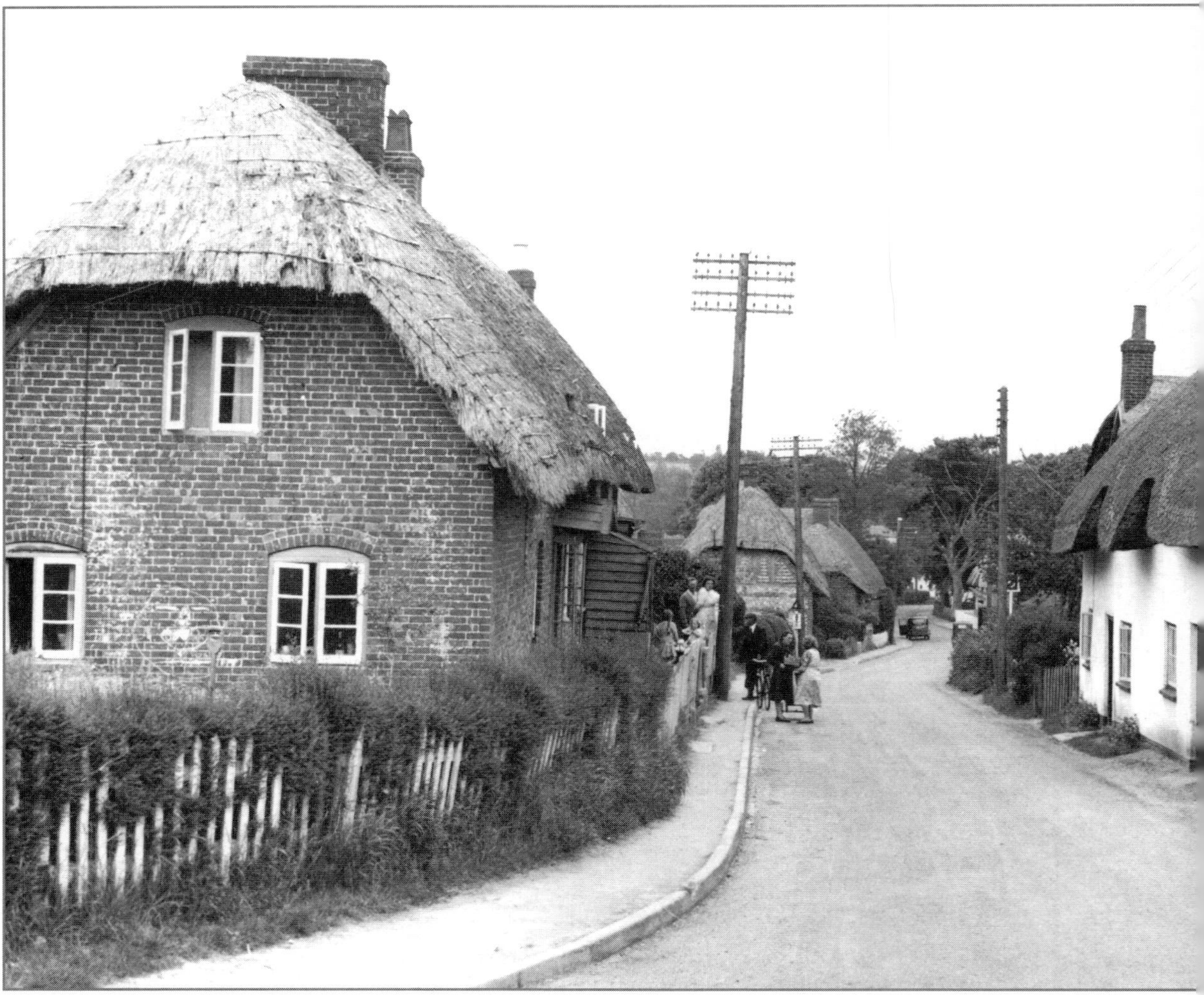

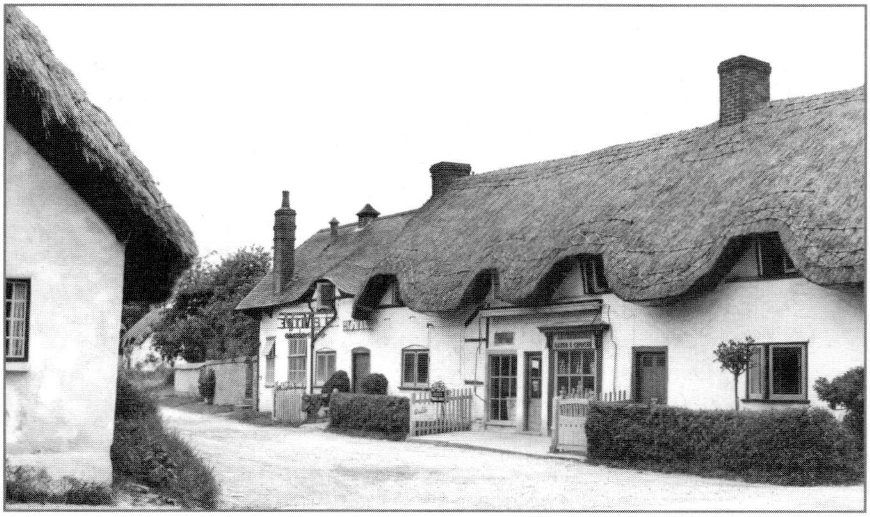

Abbotts Ann The Village Shop c1960 A4008

Here seen from the front of the Eagle Inn, soon to move to the village centre, the Village Shop and Post Office is at present part-time. The Eagle refreshes both local people and visitors and offers its skittle alley for groups.

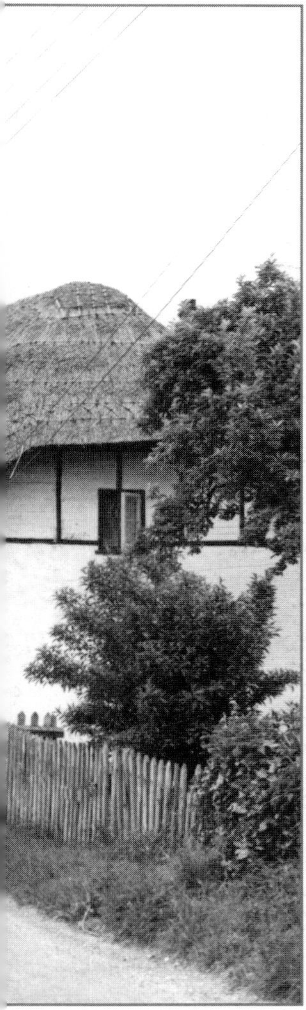

◄ **Abbotts Ann**
Red Rice Road c1955
A4004
The heart of the village retains its thatched roofs, with modern developments in pockets largely hidden from view. The Pub sign at the Eagle can just be seen beyond the power pole on the right.

▼ **Abbotts Ann**
The Village c1960 A4005
Duck Street forks to the right of the tree, Monxton Road to the left. Charles I camped near the village with a force of 5,000. On Friday, 18 October 1644, the Cavaliers of Prince Maurice's Regiment spotted the Roundheads watching them and chased them to town in the 'Battle of Andover'. Charles spent the night at the old White Hart Inn, then in Andover High Street, where the Danebury is now.

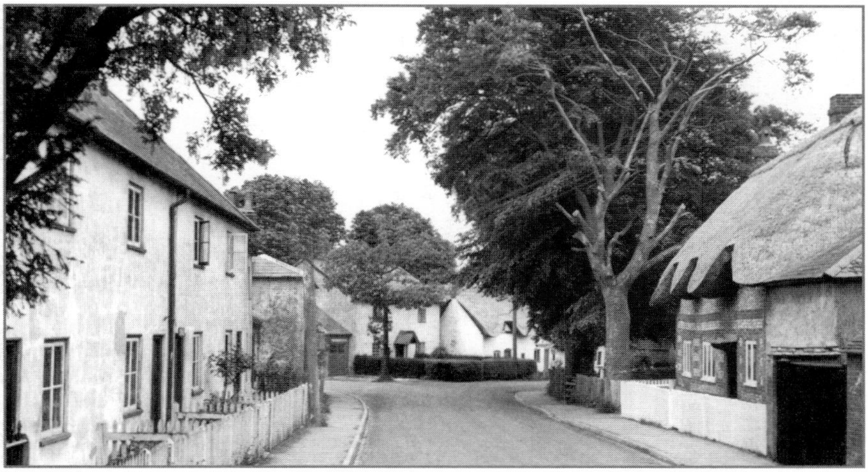

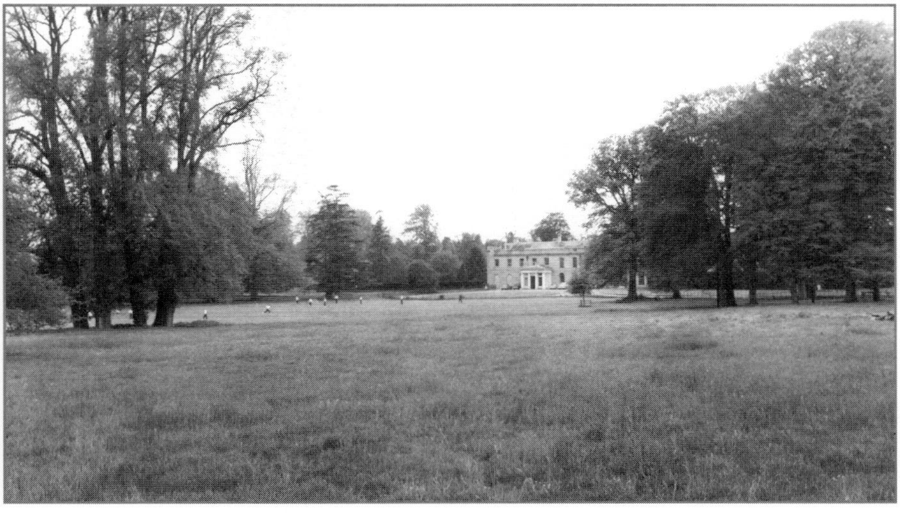

◄ **Red Rice**
Farleigh School
c1955 A53015
Red Rice House was built about 1844 and was restored in 1933 when two gate-houses were added. It replaced an earlier brick house of about 1740. The trees are said to have been laid out to show the position of the troops at Marlborough's victory at Malplaquet in 1709. The picture shows the property in its present use as a private school for boys and girls.

The Wallops, Stockbridge, Fullerton and Chilbolton

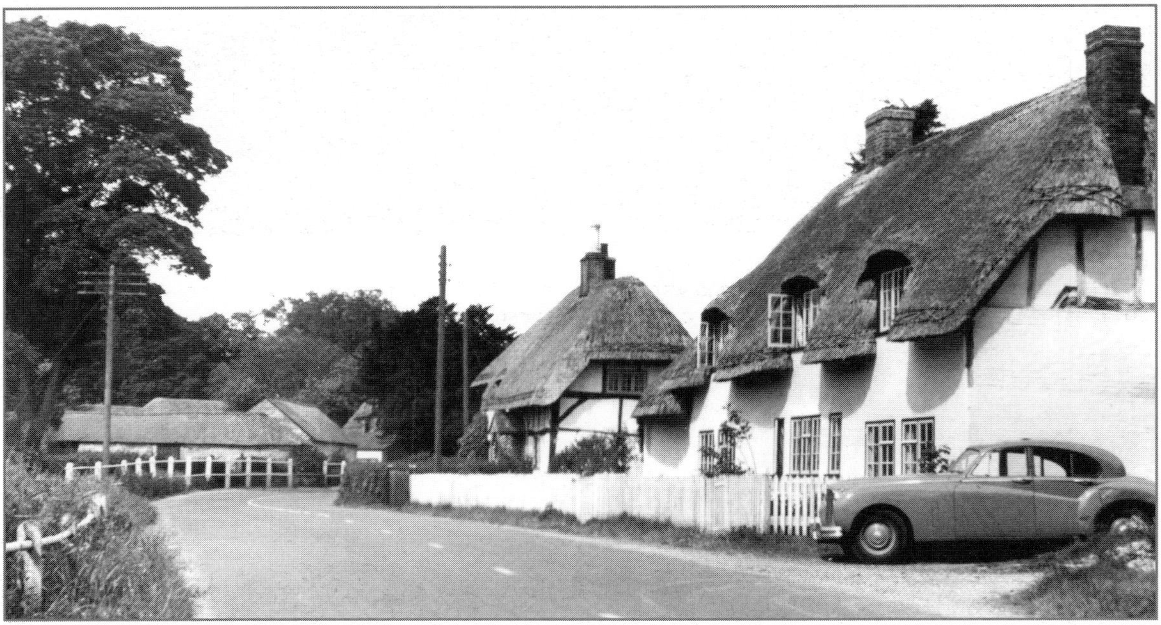

Over Wallop
The Covey c1965 O98302
The Wallop Brook flows past on the left toward Middle and Nether Wallop, behind the camera. Cottages change names from time to time but the scene remains much the same.

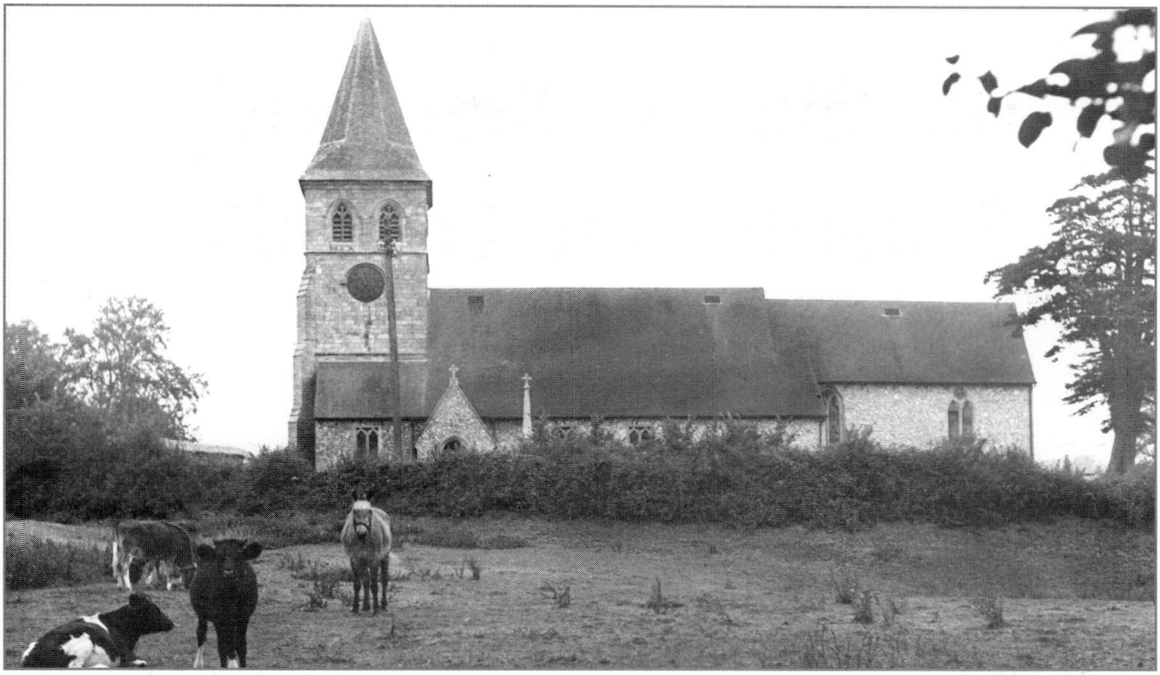

Over Wallop, St Peter's Church c1965 N156030
St Peter's was rebuilt by Pearson in 1866 and was restored in 1875. The interior has a number of Norman-style columns. The west tower with the broach spire remains as Pearson designed it.

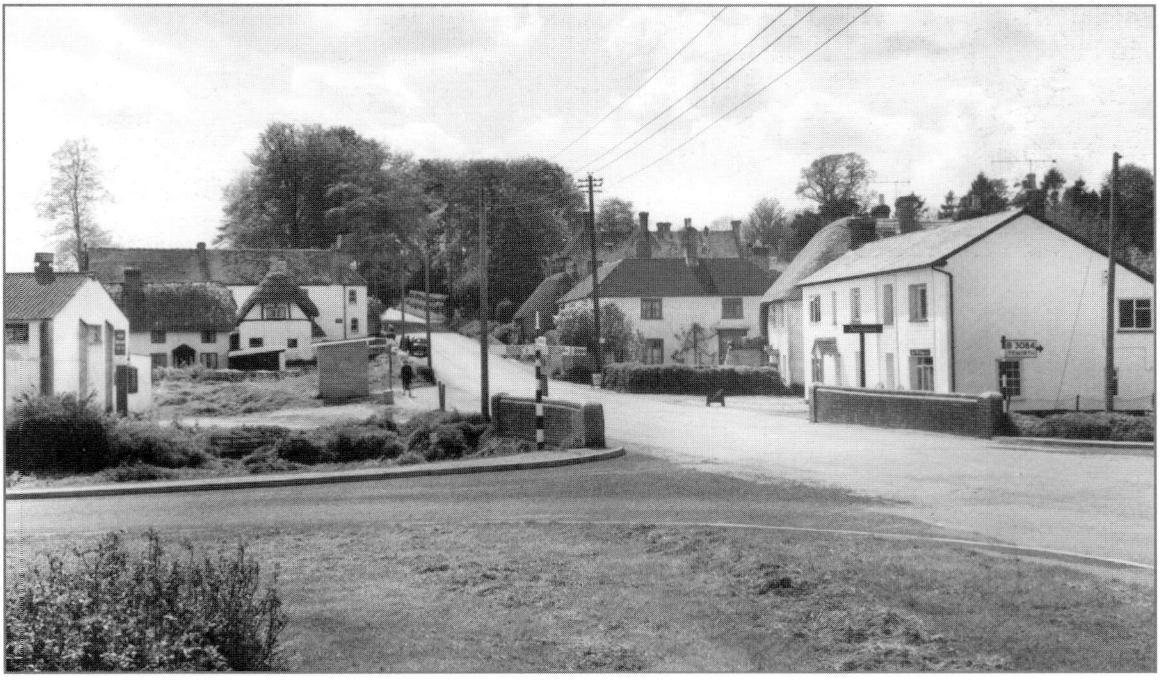

Middle Wallop, The Cross Roads c1965 M272017
Middle Wallop is a village of at least twenty-six houses with a garage, a pub and an army airfield. But it has no sign to welcome the visitor, as parishes pay for the signs, and Middle Wallop is in the parish of Nether Wallop.

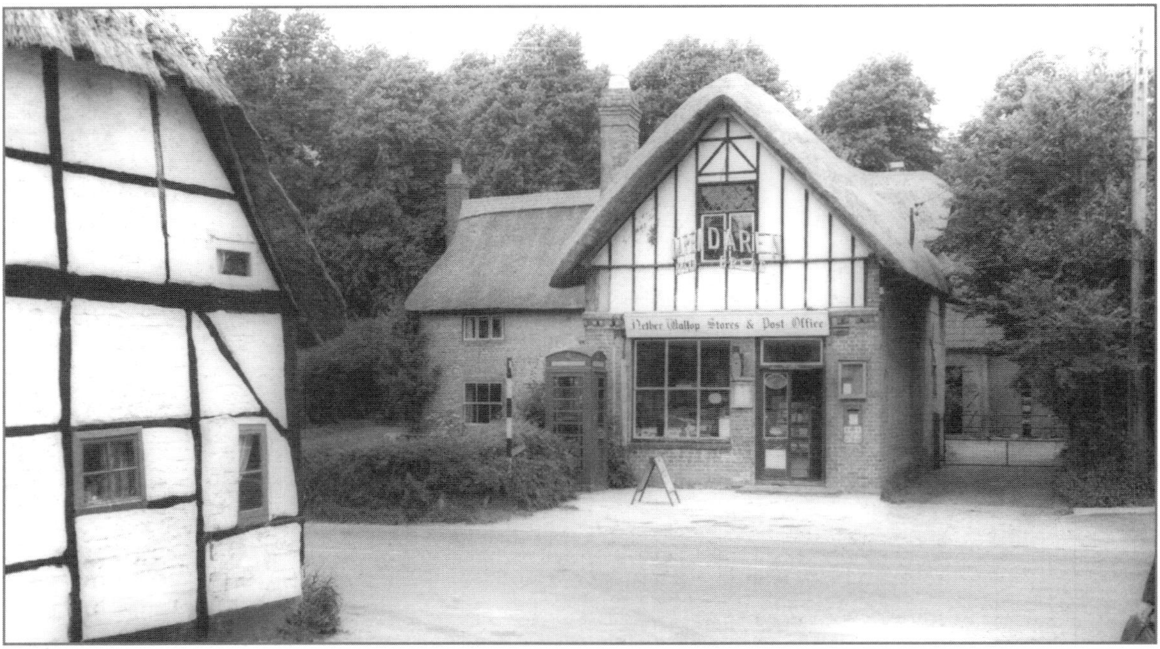

Nether Wallop, Stores and Post Office c1965 N156019
Here once was Nether Wallop Village Store and Post Office. Now it is a house and a tiny plate above the shop window reads 'The Old Post Office'. Four half days a week, the Village Hall hosts the Post Office. A few things may be bought at the Trout Shop by the Old Mill.

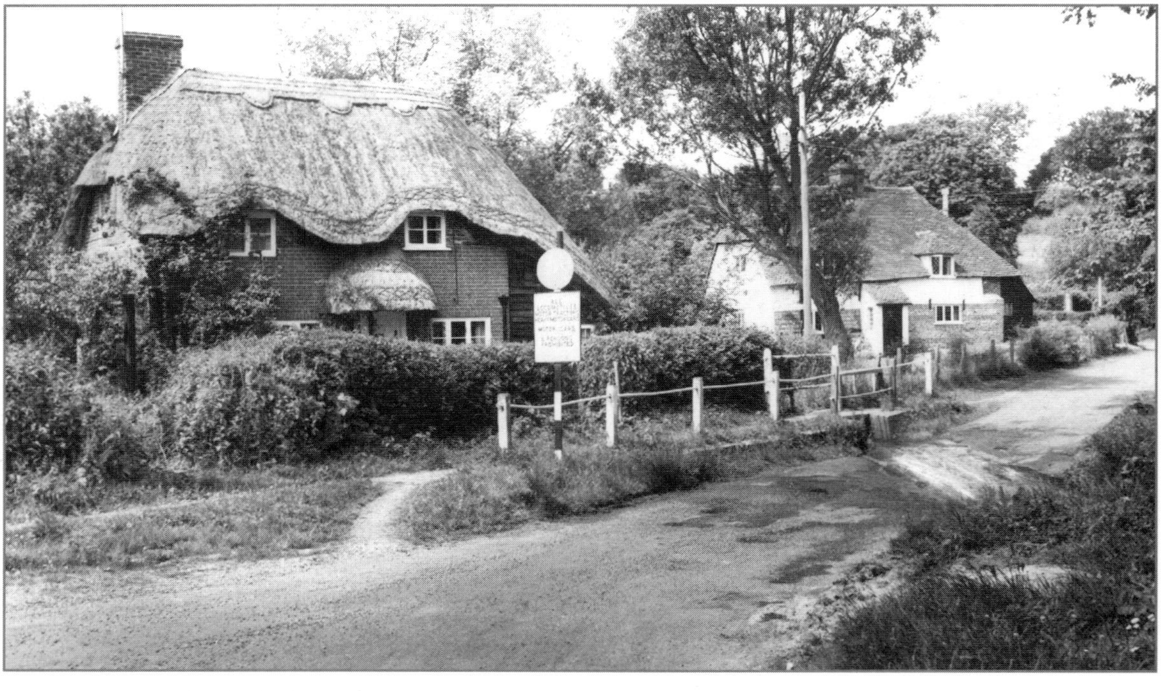

Nether Wallop, The Splash c1960 N156023
The Splash still flows but the hedging has grown high on the left. Dancing Green Cottage is almost hidden, but Blenheim Cottage is still to be seen.

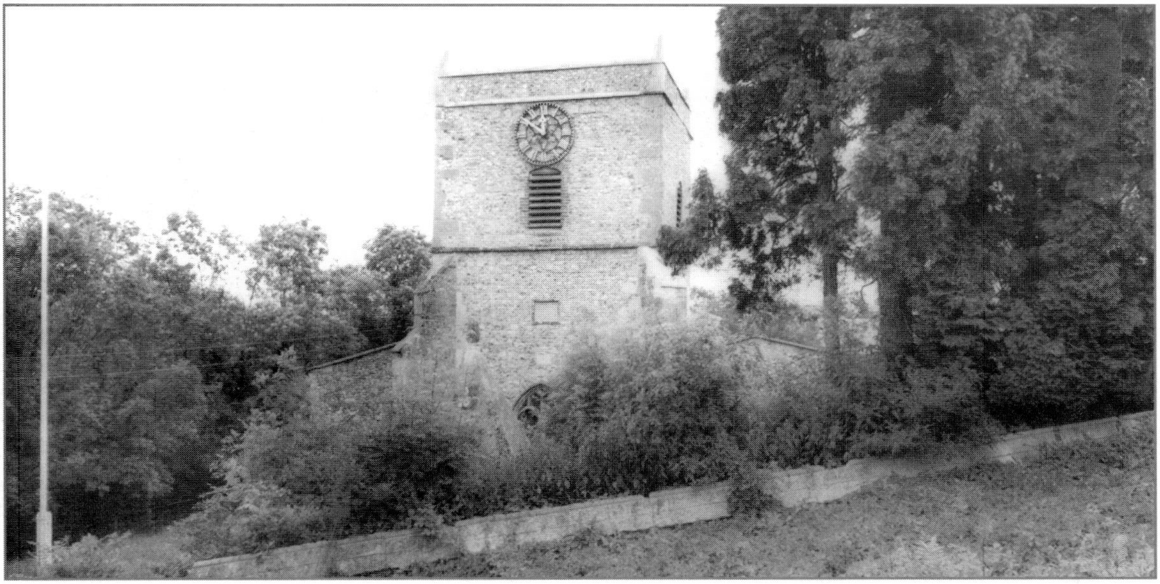

Nether Wallop, St Andrew's Church c1965 N156017

The Church of St Andrew is special. In the centre is the original church of about 960, which consisted of a nave and a chancel with choir stalls and an 1880 organ. The church extends in all directions. The choir arch and several nave bays carry remnants of Medieval paintings. The tower of 1756 records churchwardens and masons. Of interest is the tomb of local benefactor, 'Francis Douce, Doctor of Physick', who died in 1759 and was buried under a pyramid beyond the tower.

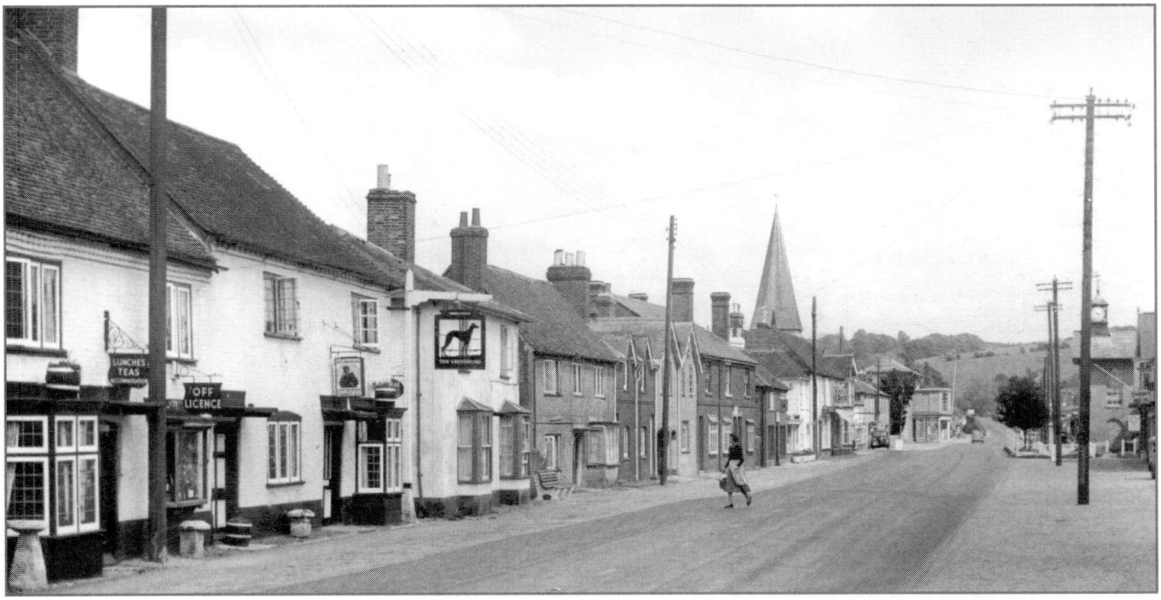

Stockbridge, The Greyhound c1955 S259064

Visitors to the tourist attraction of Stockbridge enter downhill at either end of the High Street. Almost a mile long, it runs east-west, with narrow ribbons of houses on either side. Only recently has development begun in well-concealed pockets. It is said that the Romans used bundles of faggots to strengthen the ancient peaty way. Sheep could be rested and watered in the valley before resuming the drove to Weyhill Fair.

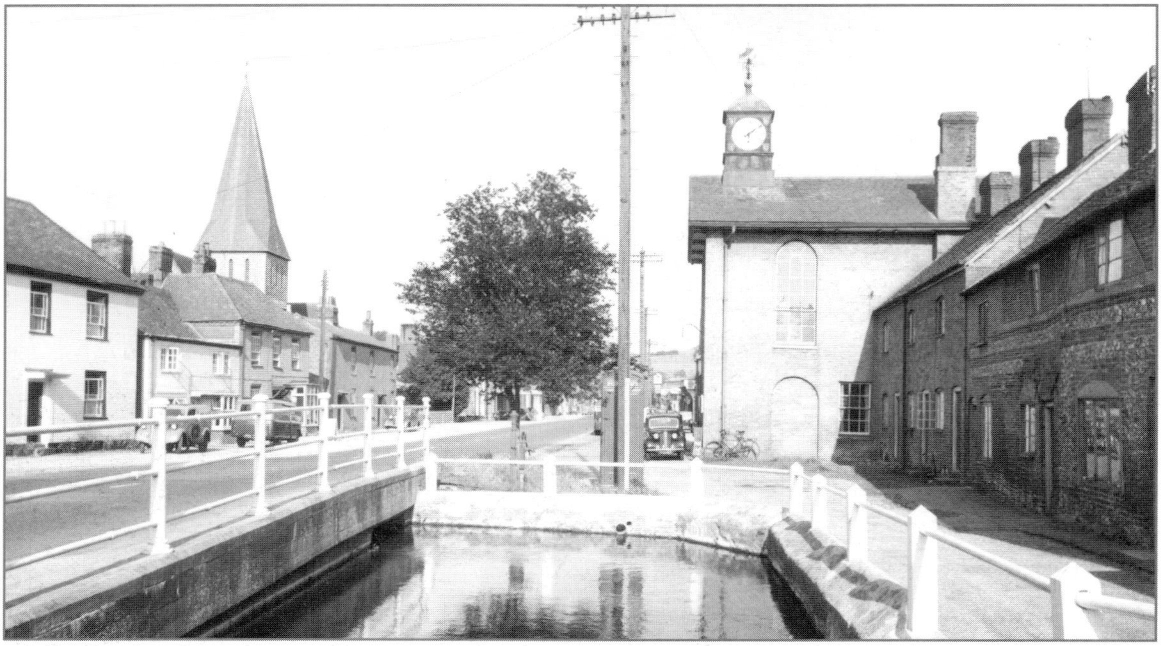

Stockbridge, High Street c1955 S259074
The Test is famous for excellent fishing. At this waterway, 30 or 40 brown trout often swim under the ducks. The Georgian Town Hall of 1810 regularly holds antiques auctions and the town is well-known as an antiques centre with plenty of shops in which to browse. St Peter's Church Spire is the landmark further on.

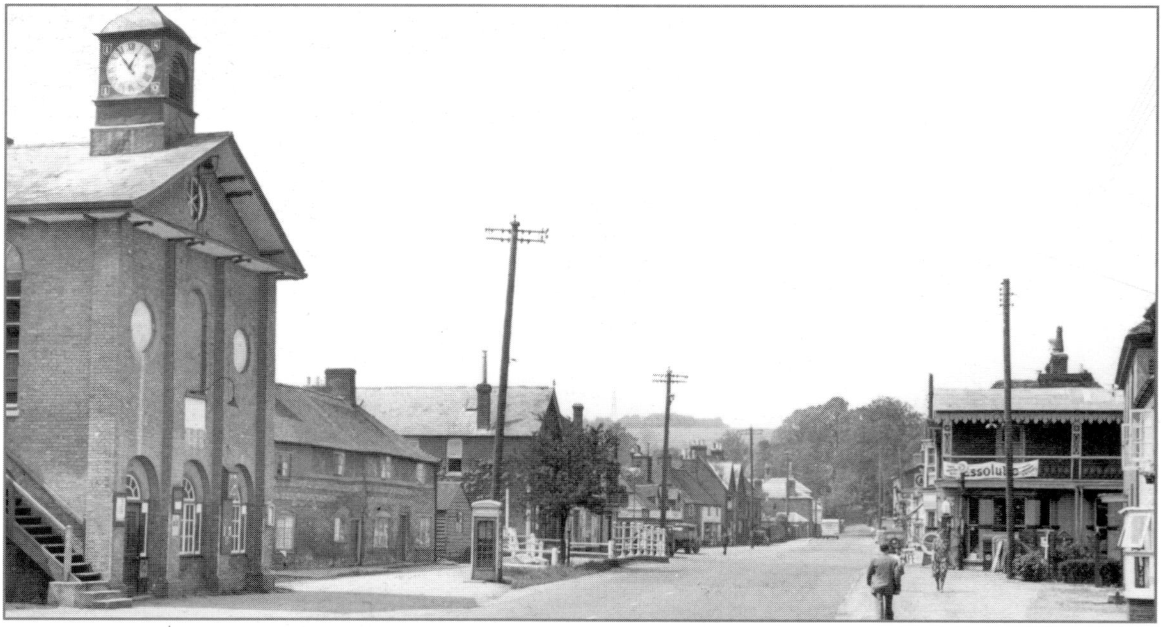

Stockbridge, High Street c1955 S259049
19th-century race days on Danebury Downs brought many keen race-goers to Stockbridge, including Edward VII and Lily Langtry. Shops and eating houses would be bustling. Excellent cakes were on sale from a nearby bakery and painted ladies in their bustles and boas would drape the veranda (where the garage is now). The races are gone; only a hint of the past lingers in Lillie's Bakery and Tearoom.

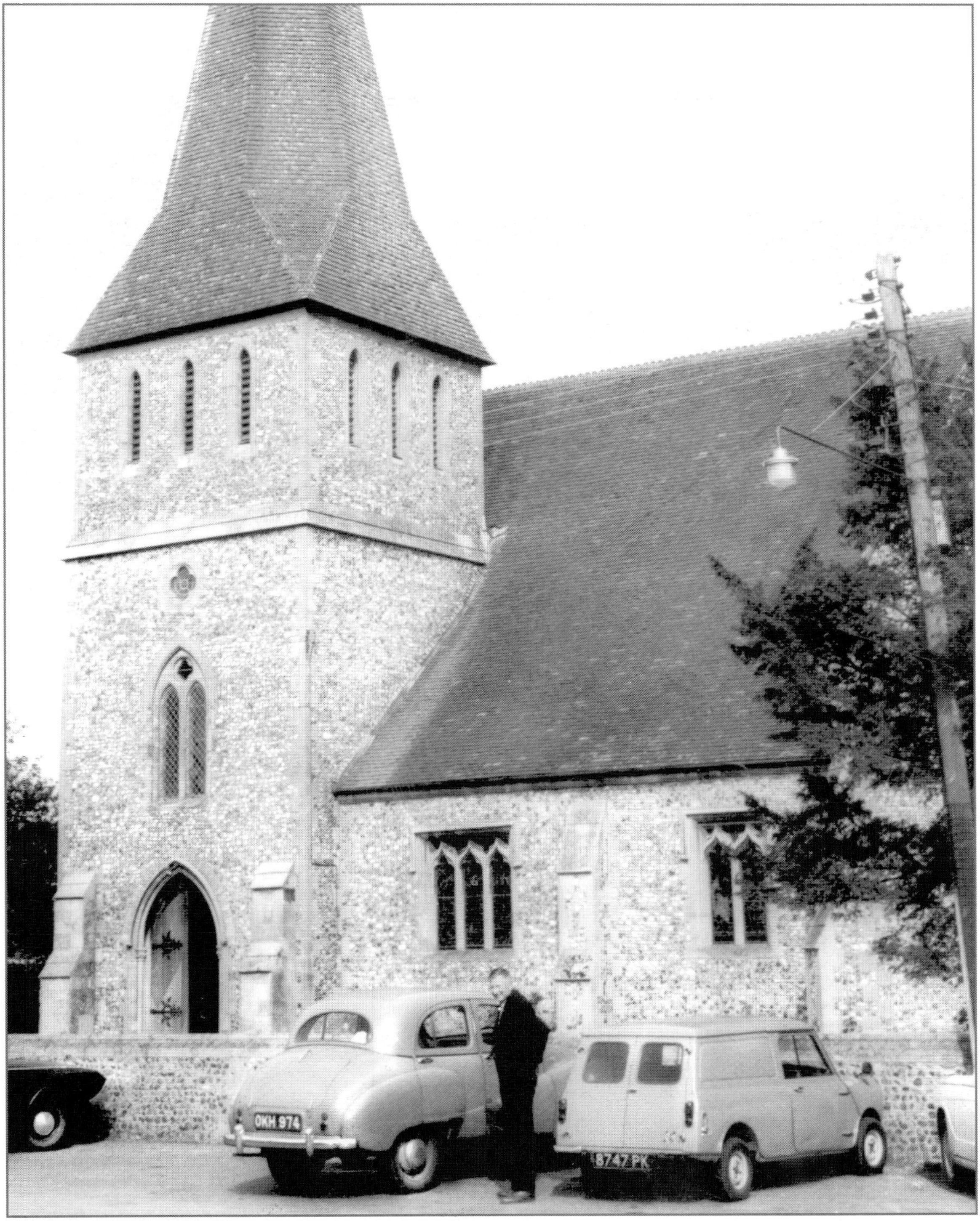

Stockbridge, St Peter's Church c1965 S259099
Old St Peter's became too small as the town expanded west. A site in the centre of town was found for the new church which was built in 1866 incorporating some old windows. The steeple was added in 1887. The north arcade is said to be special.

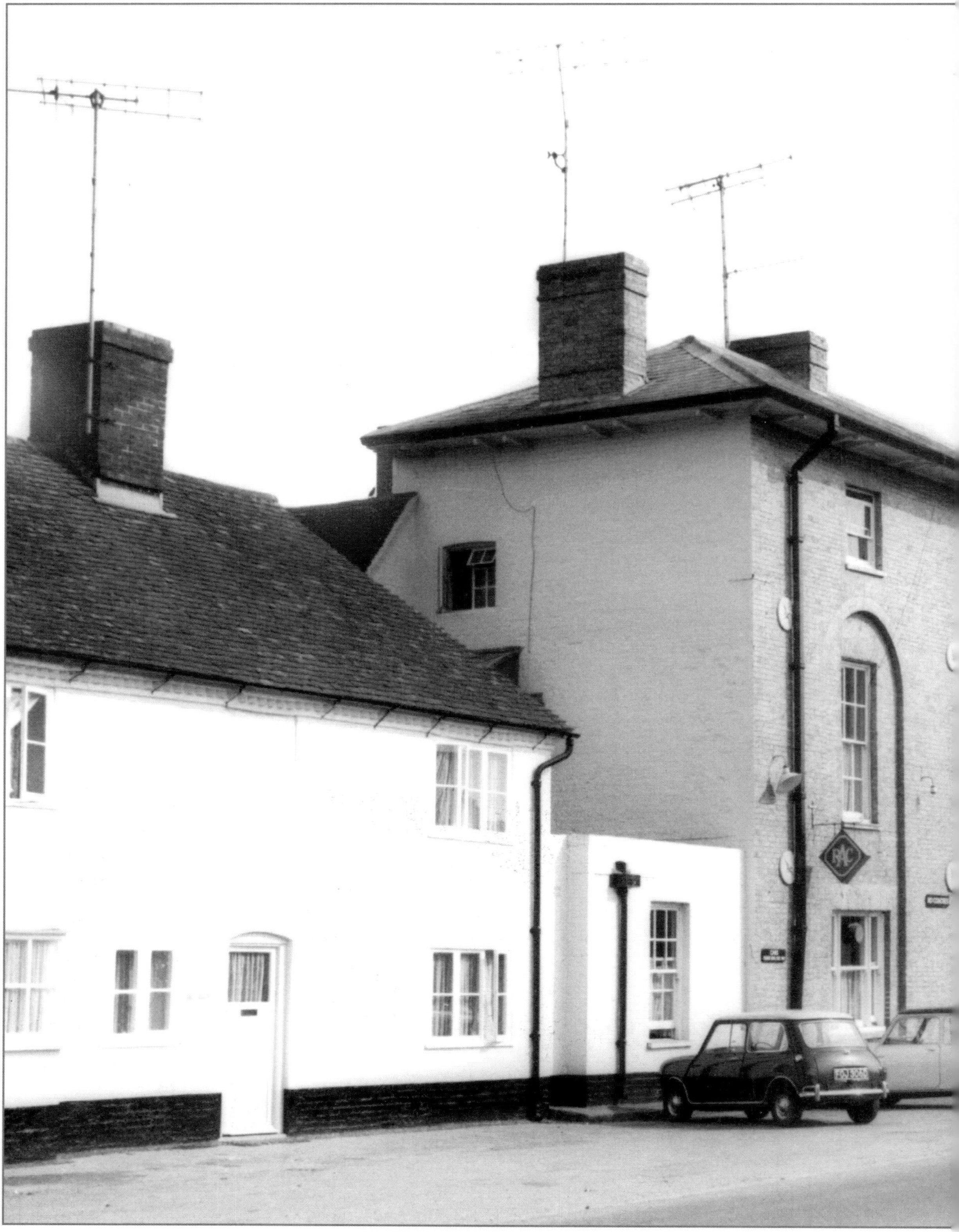

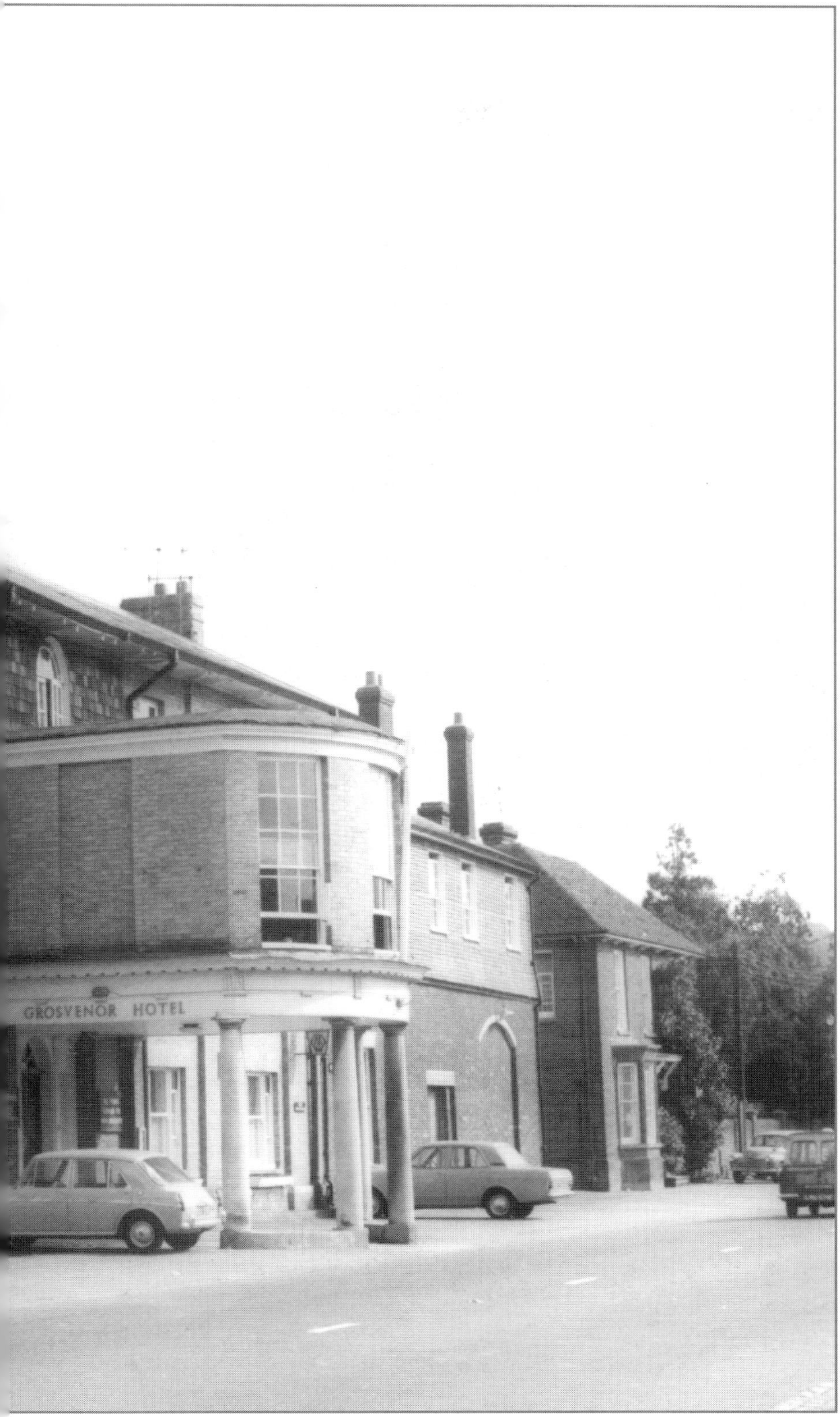

Stockbridge
The Grosvenor Hotel
c1965 S259098

A 'porte cochere', overhanging the pavement, served two functions in coaching days: those in the coach could alight and keep dry, while travellers on top and the luggage could enter the building by a high level door. Coach days have gone but the hotel is still busy. Here on the porte cochere with the best view of the High Street, is the renowned Houghton Fishing Club's meeting room.

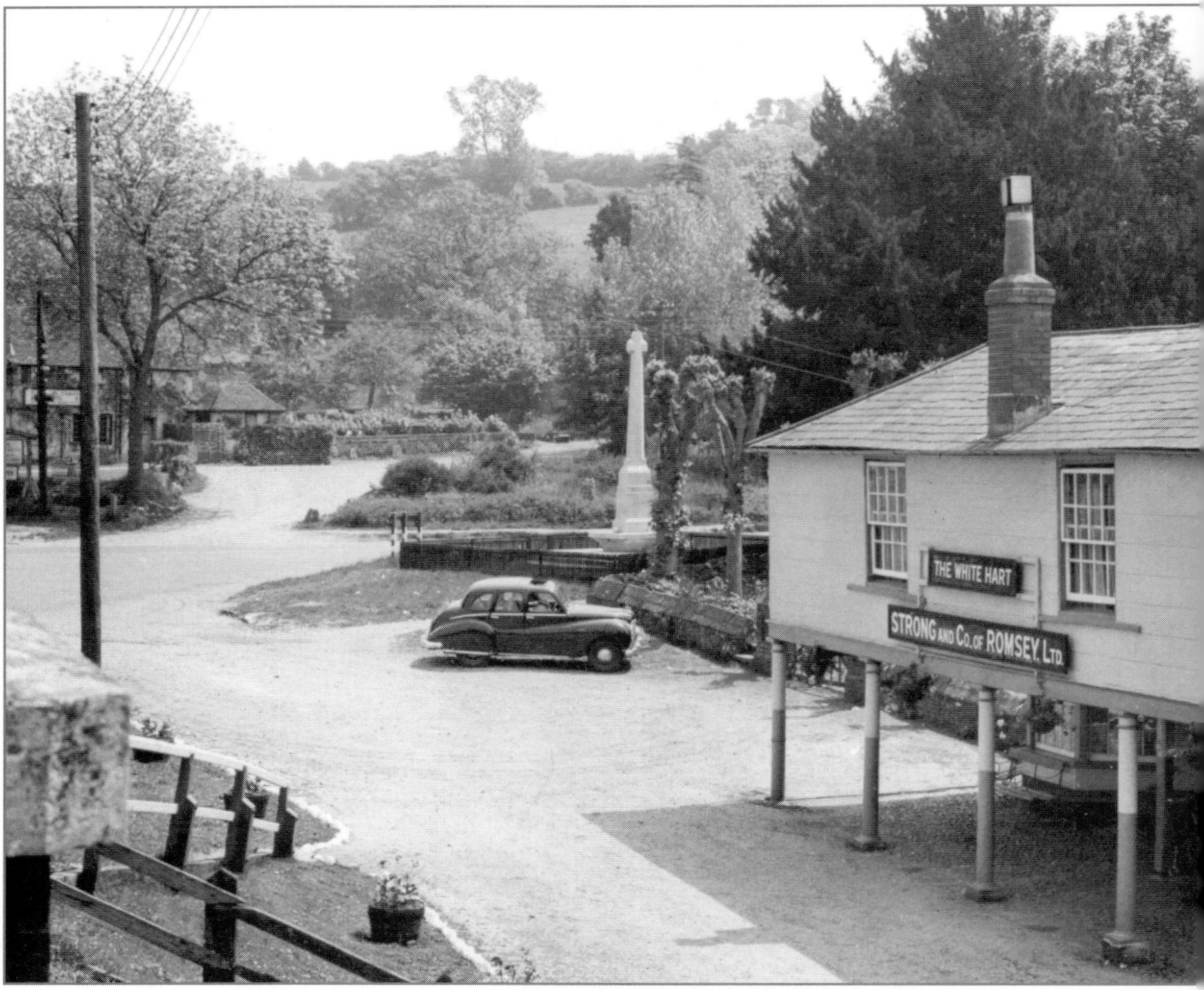

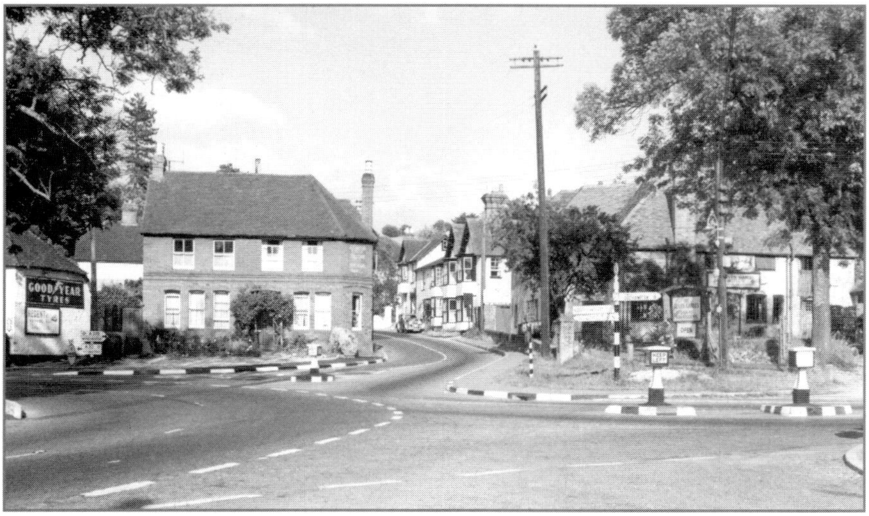

◄ **Stockbridge**
The Old Andover Road
c1955 S259068

To the right, Winchester Road rises to leave town; to the left it enters town. The road forward has been a cul-de-sac since Lord Beeching closed the railway in 1964, giving room for a by-pass to Andover and Basingstoke and the roundabout now facing The White Hart Inn.

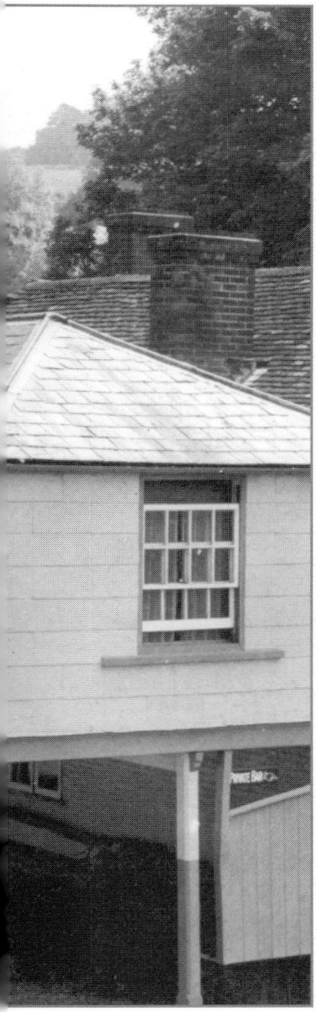

Stockbridge The White Hart Inn c1955 S259053

Today's roundabout leaves no trace of the railway and bridge from which this bird's eye view was taken. The Inn has since prospered and the garden has expanded. The War Memorial can be seen behind the car. Old St Peter's 12th-century church hides behind the inn.

Stockbridge Marsh Court c1955 S259055

The sunshine picks out the white walls of rock chalk of this fine Edwardian house designed by Sir Edwin Lutyens with planting and landscaping by Gertrude Jekyll. Built as a private house in 1904, it was a private school for many years and reverted to country house use in the 1980s. An amazing table was cut in the virgin chalk and finished on top as the billiard table above the sunken floor.

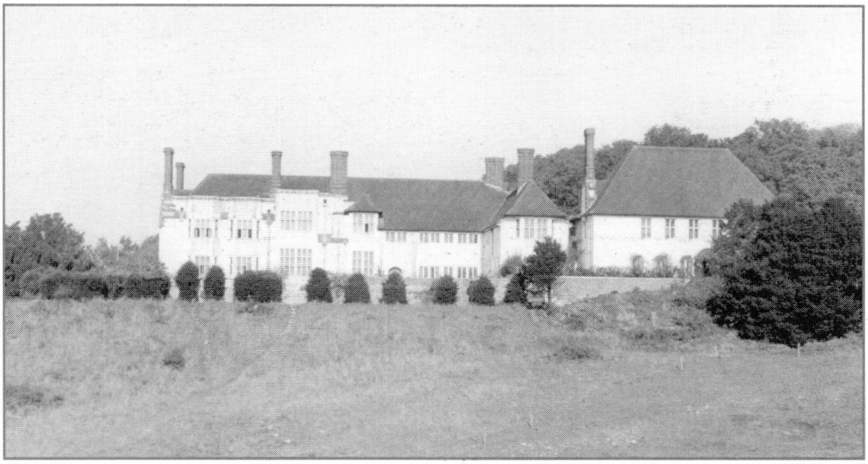

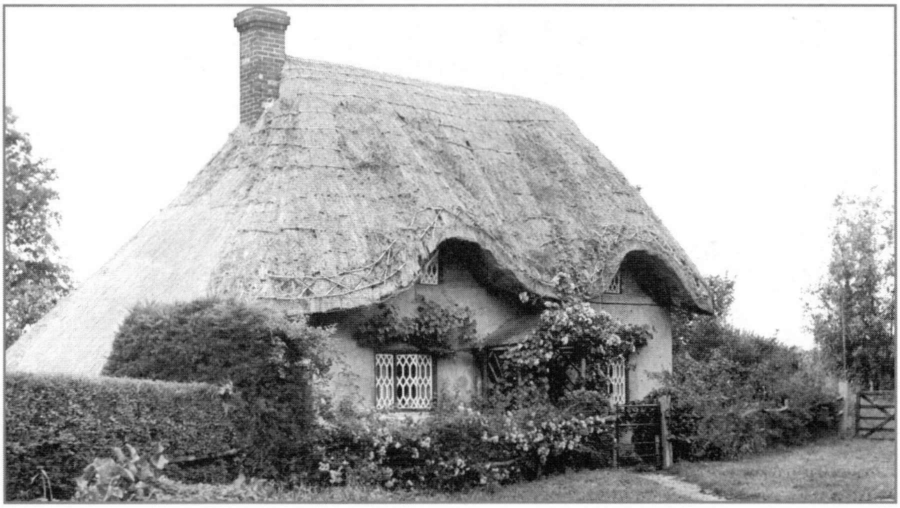

Fullerton Vine Cottage c1960 F109004

Viewed from the old railway bridge, here is Vine Cottage by the River Anton where it joins the Test is at Fullerton Junction. Here the single line track divided left for Andover, right to follow the Test to Wherwell, Longparish, Hurstbourne Priors and then to the London main line. With no smoky tunnels, Queen Victoria's favourite railway line was just like 'going down the Nile'.

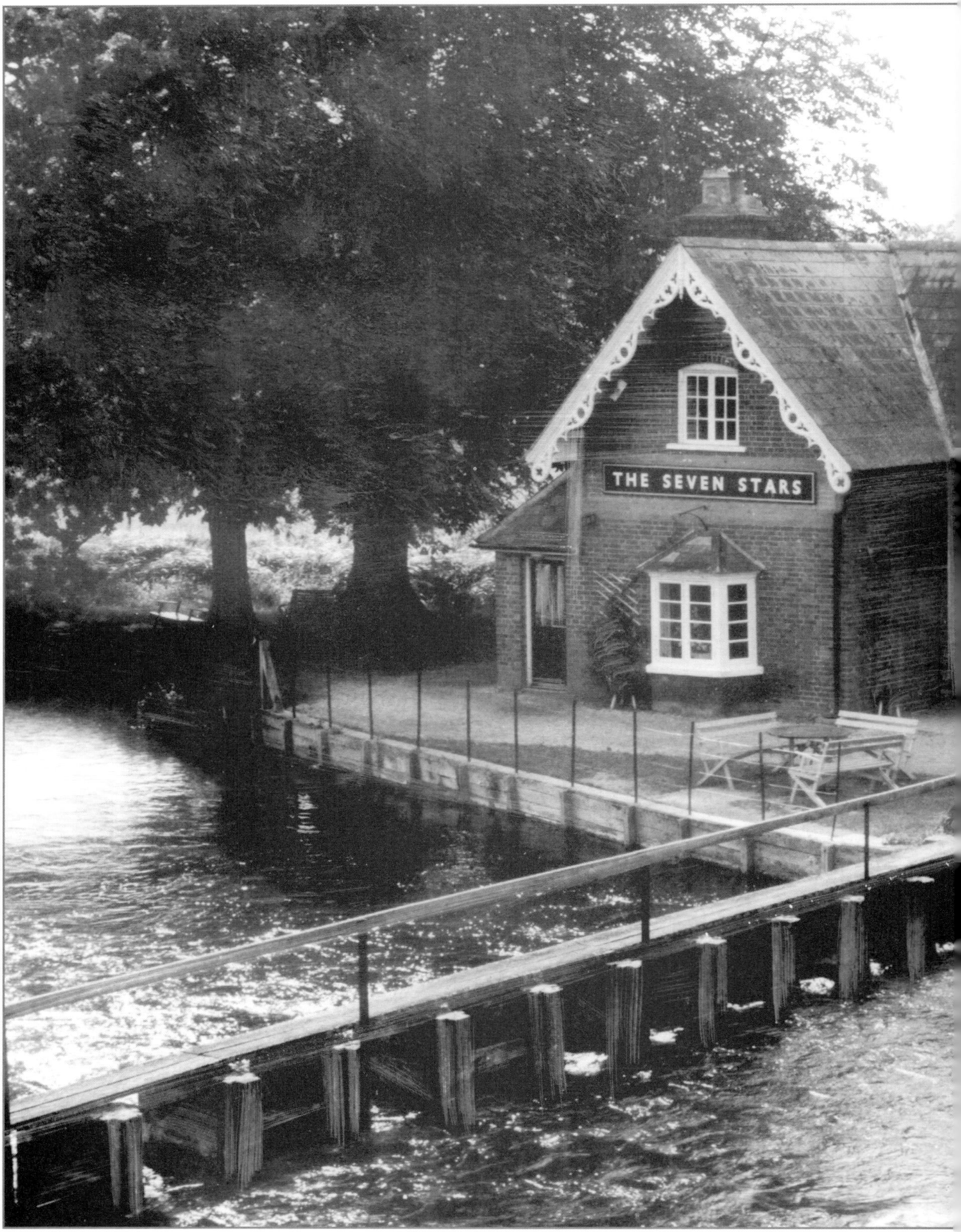
THE SEVEN STARS

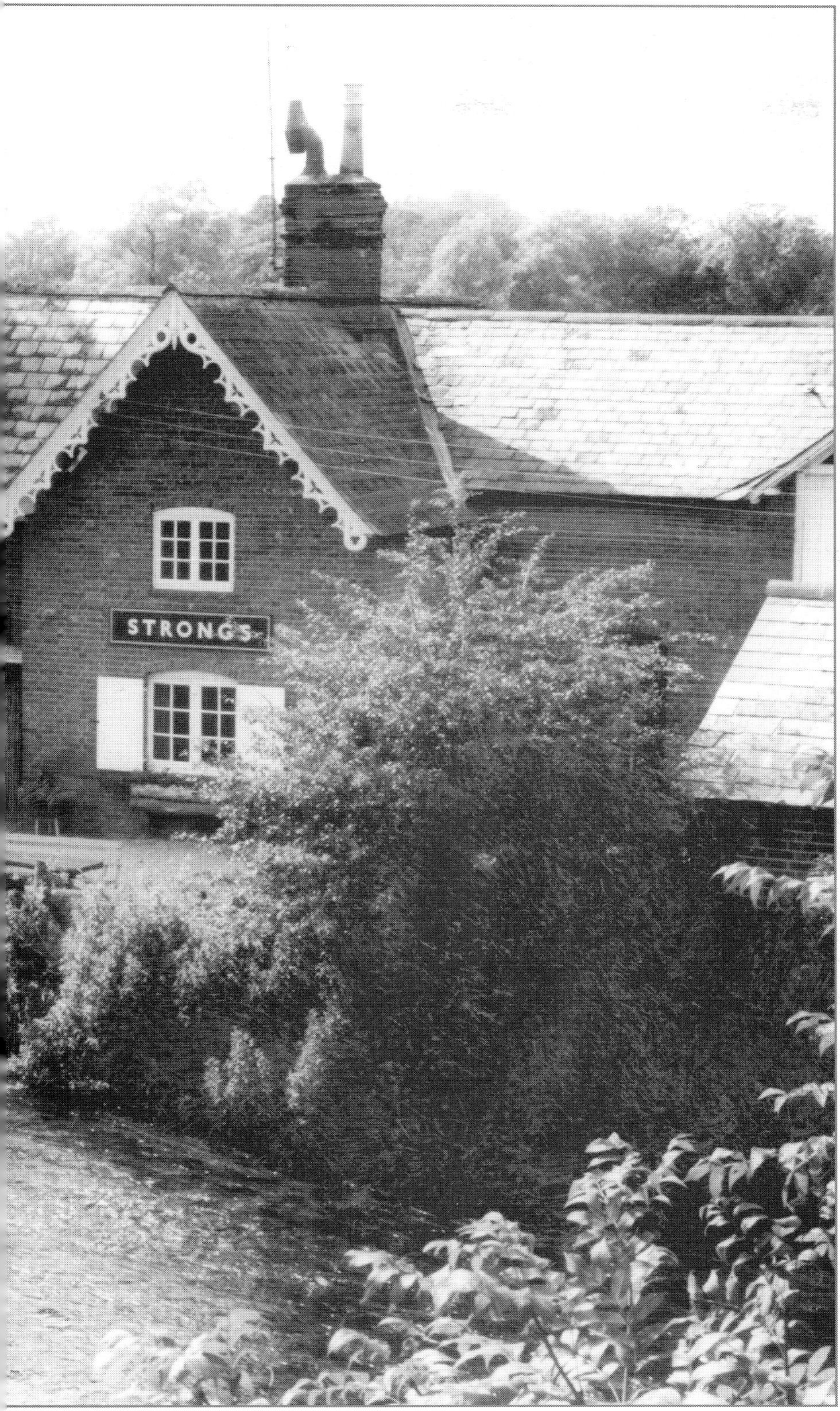

Chilbolton
The Seven Stars
c1960 C227020

Before reaching Chilbolton Village, here is the Seven Stars Public House and the beautiful River Test, viewed from the bridge. Across the water was once the railway. The Mayfly (as it is now) is still the perfect place to sit outside, watching passing trout and enjoying a refreshment or good meal.

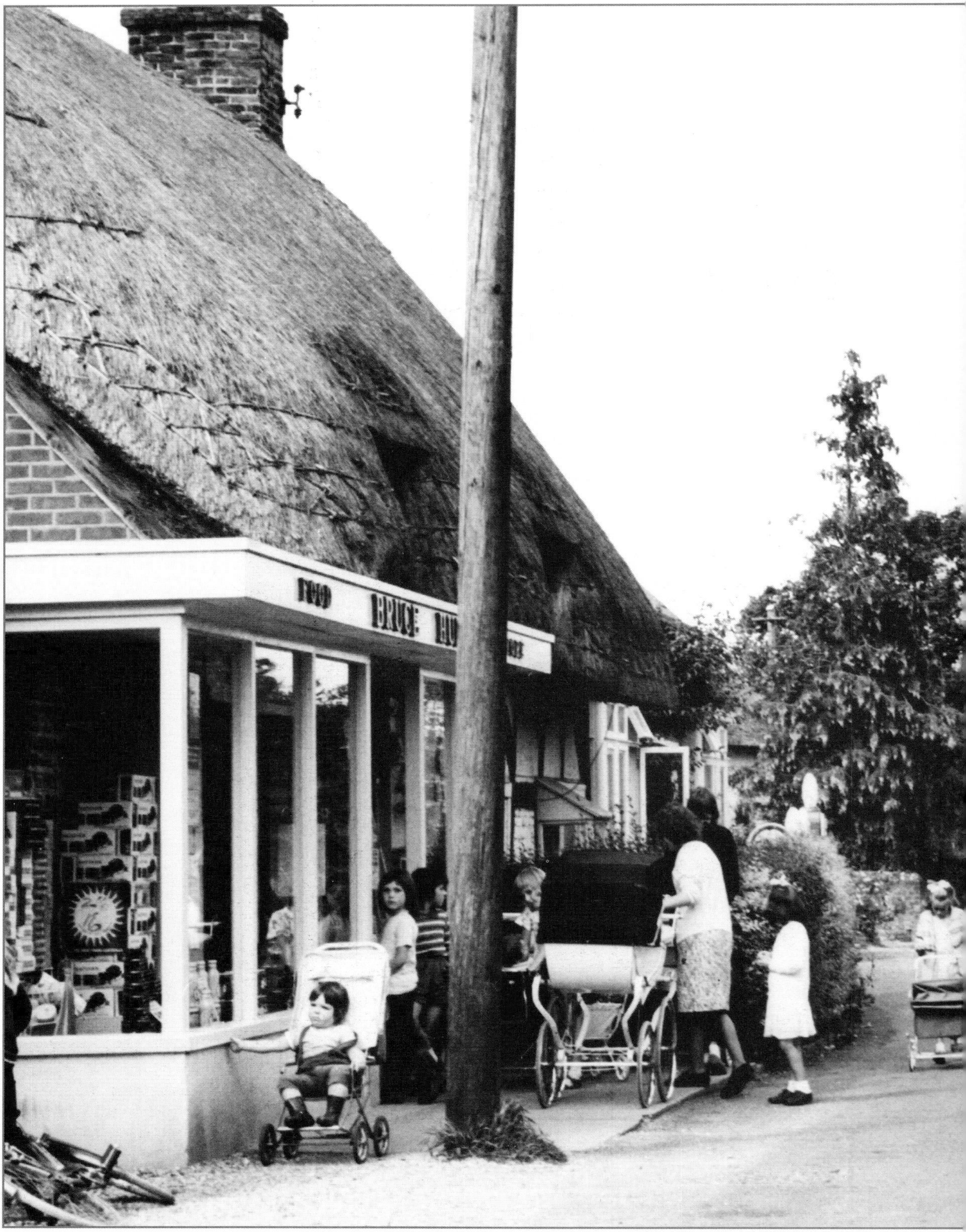

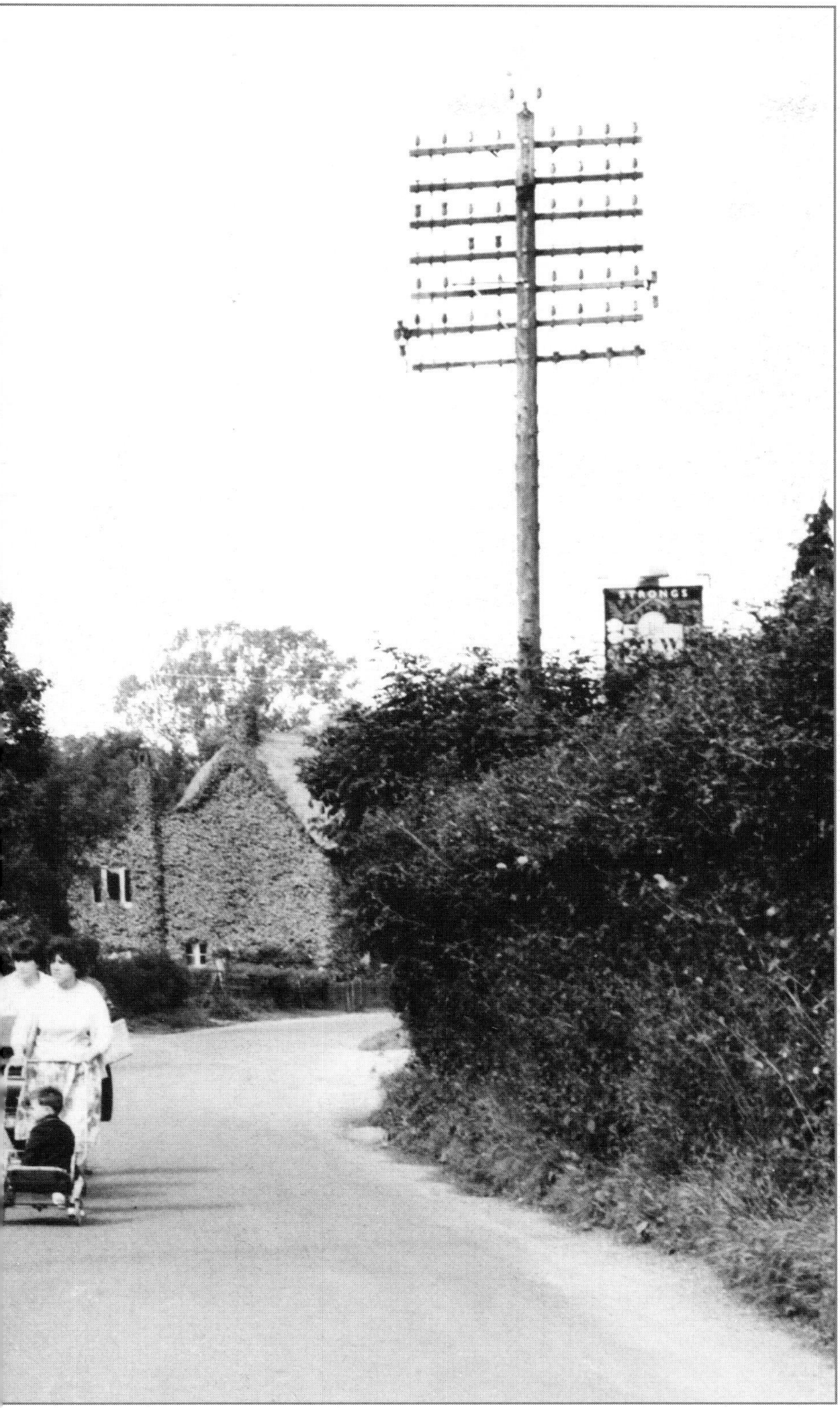

Chilbolton
High Street c1965
C227018
The sign of the Abbott's Mitre pokes up over the hedge, beckoning with refreshment and food. The Village Shop and Post Office serve the village six days a week.

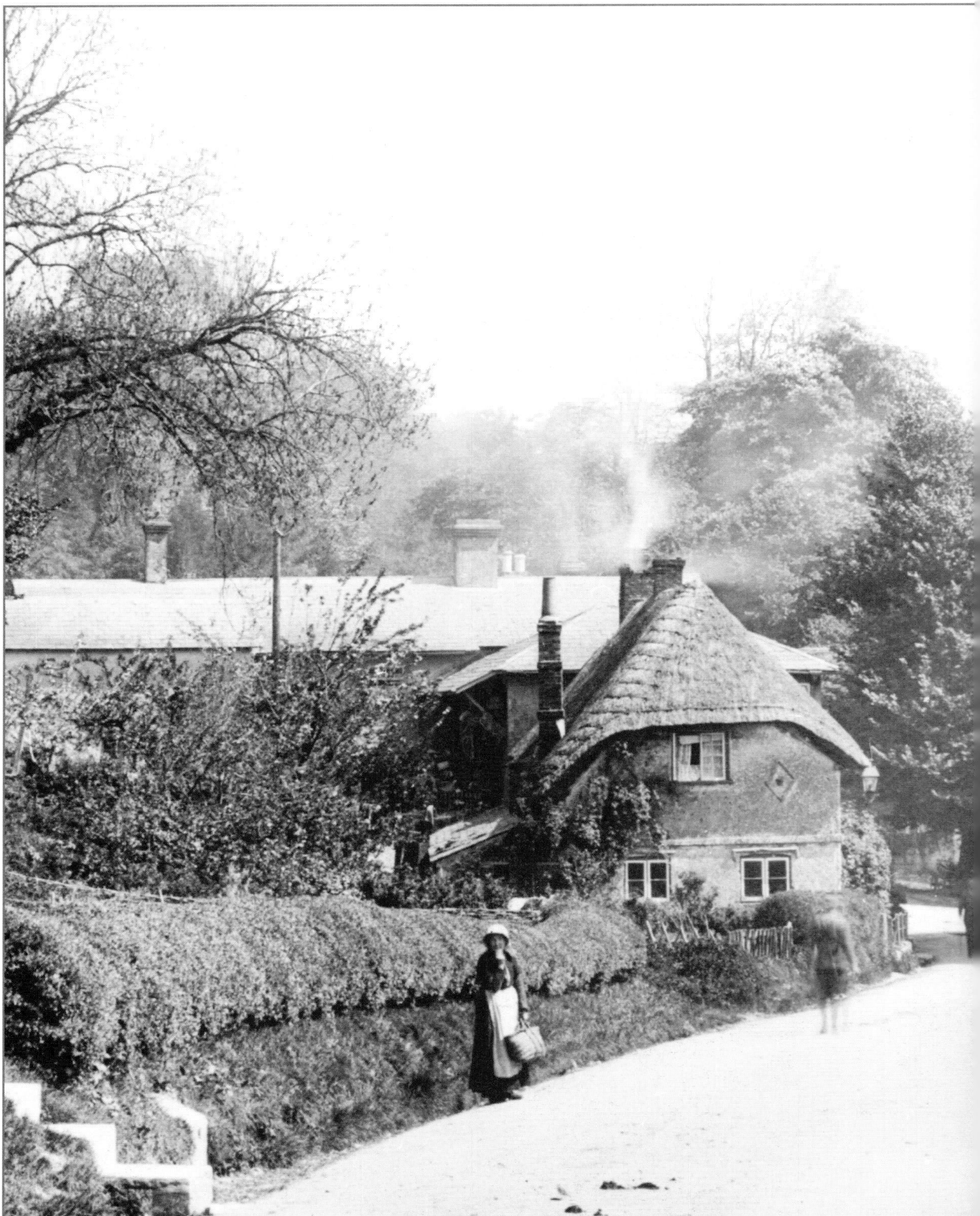

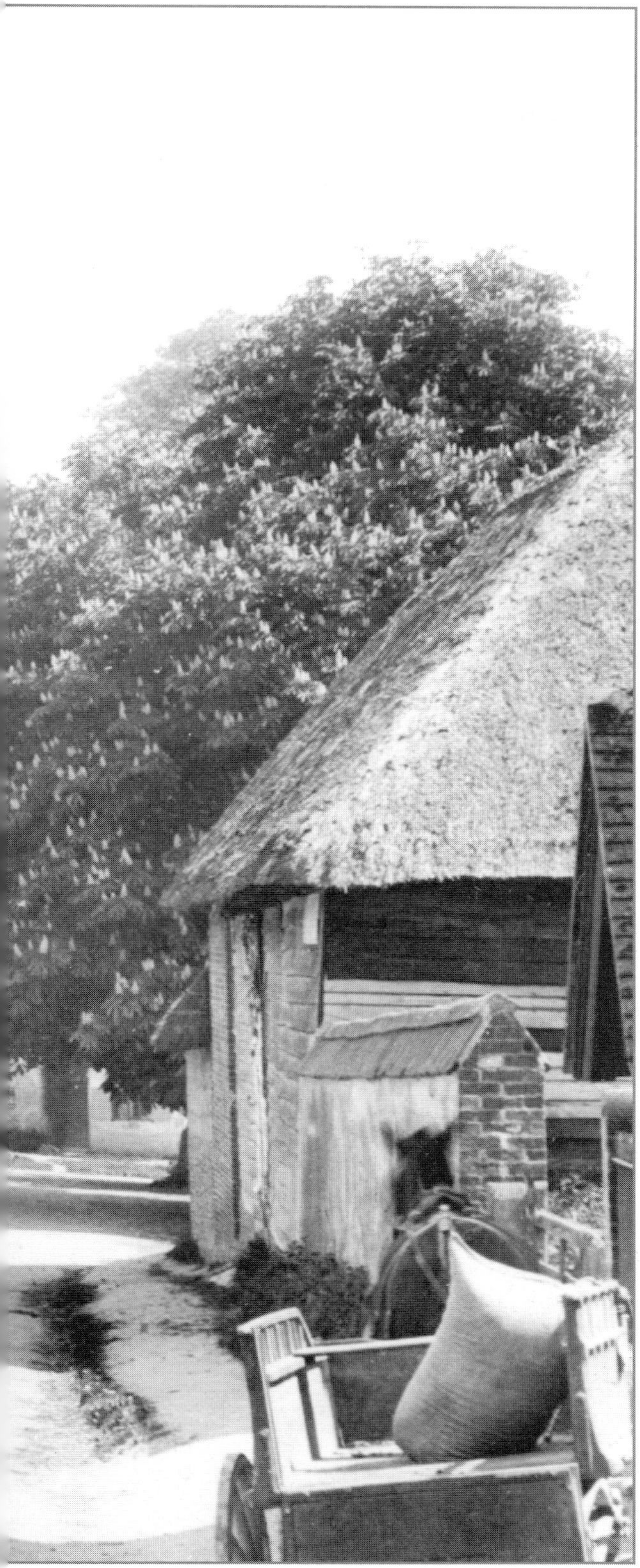

Wherwell, the Clatfords and Anna Valley

Wherwell, High Street 1901 46353
This could almost be Wherwell today. In the 1940s, Mrs Chadwick's tearoom gave servicemen teas under Chestnut Cottage's thatch. Behind the tearoom, the Village Shop, now closed, was once an inn with stables and yard running back from the road. On the right the old farmyard and barns recently became Kingsmill Barns and Cottages. This scene reflects a time before the First World War, now marked by the Great War Memorial at the road junction.

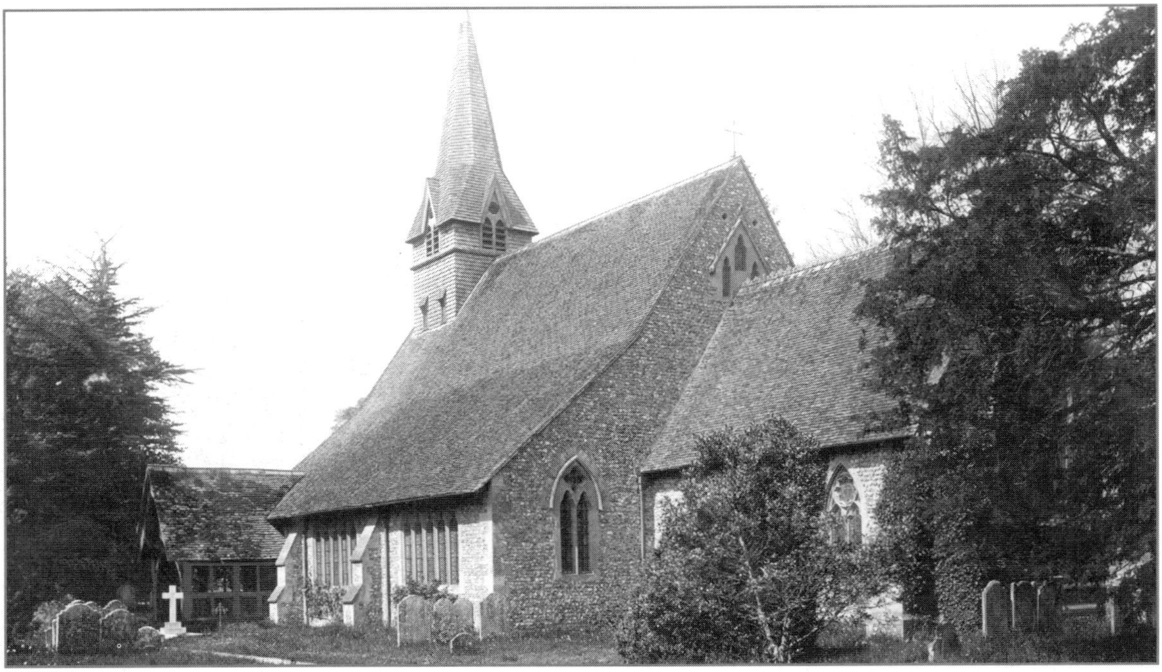

Wherwell, The Church of St Peter and Holy Cross 1901 46355

Rebuilt in 1856-8 on a medieval site, this church has fragments from the old church on display. The architect was Woodyer of Guildford, and the builder, Holdaway from Wherwell. An inscription reads, '1691 Purchased of the Right Honbl John Ld La-War By Philadephia Whitehead out of Ye Yearly Rent of The White Lion Inn in Wherwill the Sum of Twelve Shillings to be paid yearly to Twelve old Men and Women at Christmas for ever'. What confidence in the future!

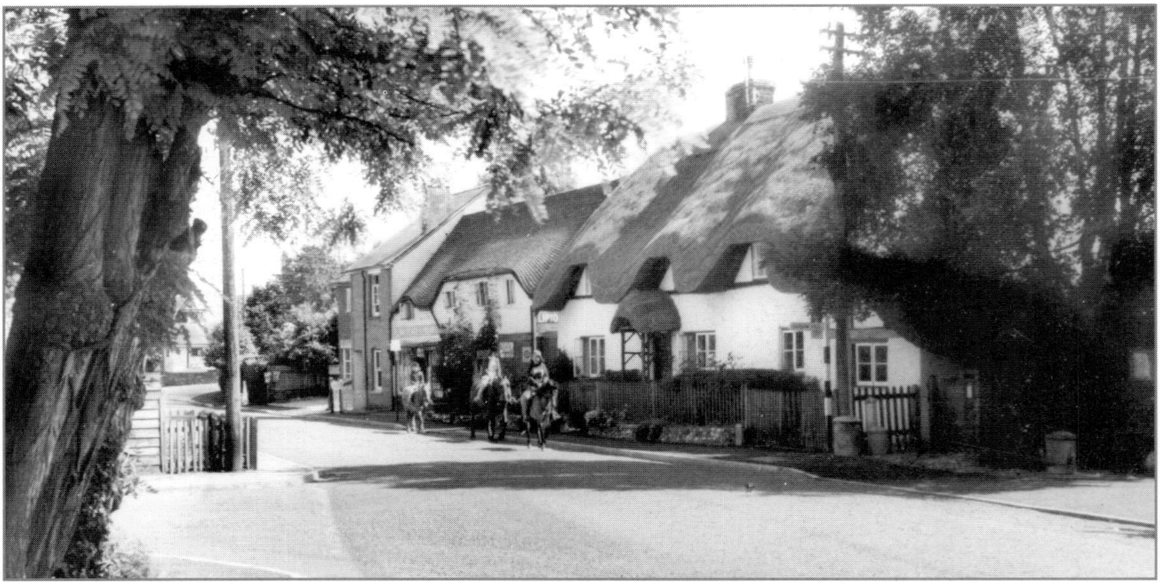

Goodworth Clatford, The Village c1965 G87001

The ponies have just passed the shop which closed a few years ago. Now the Bee Hive Store and Post Office have been built at the end of the terrace and provide service six and a half days a week. Hampshire villages are much in demand and sites coming to market are usually rare. Barrow Hill runs off to the left with modern houses. Just a mile or so up-river, Upper Clatford has the same appeal.

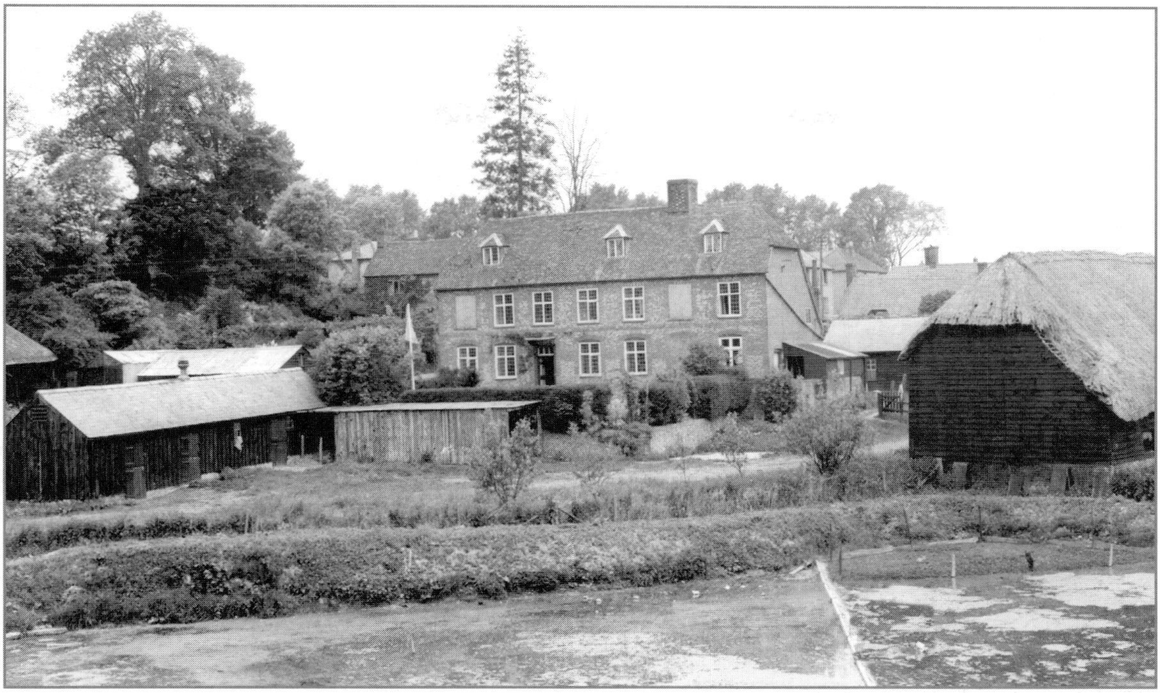

Upper Clatford, Sackville Court Farm c1955 U53002
The view here from the old railway bridge has greatly been changed from 1955. The farmyard is now expansive lawn and garden. Trees now almost entirely hide the house from view. The pond is swept and tamed by weeping willows.

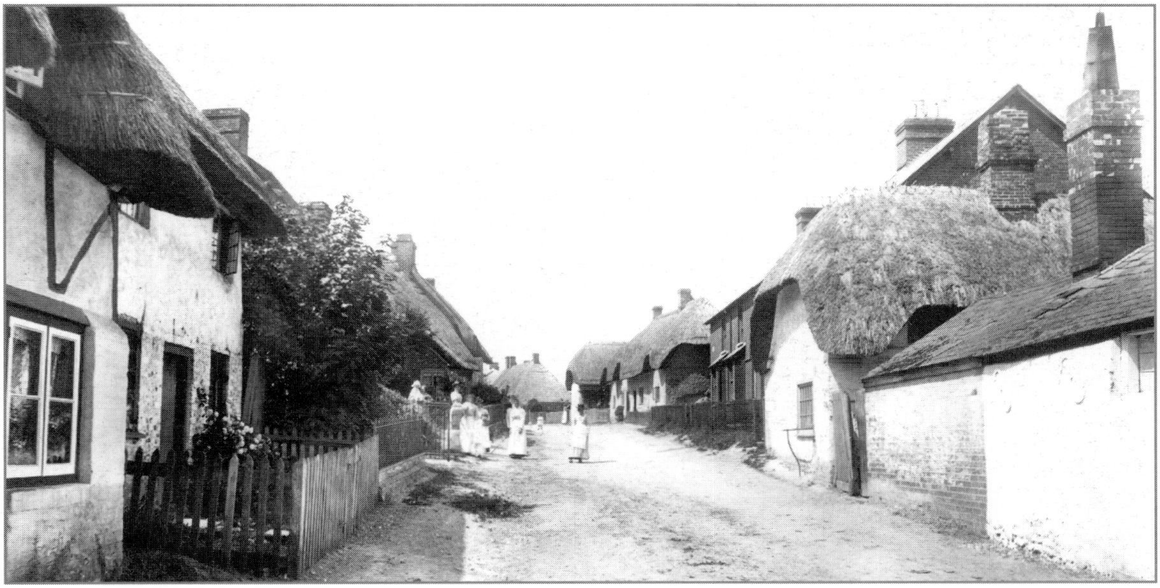

Upper Clatford, The Village 1899 43693
Far left is the dining room of today's Crook and Shears. A modern house, the White House, replaced the building next door. Behind the ladies are 1-3 Beddles Cottages, which still stand. On the near right, the Moorings has now changed its thatch for slate. Slate-roofed Anchor View and Lee View, built in 1888, still remain, although the two distant cottages have now gone. Chalfont Cottage would eventually lose its thatch.

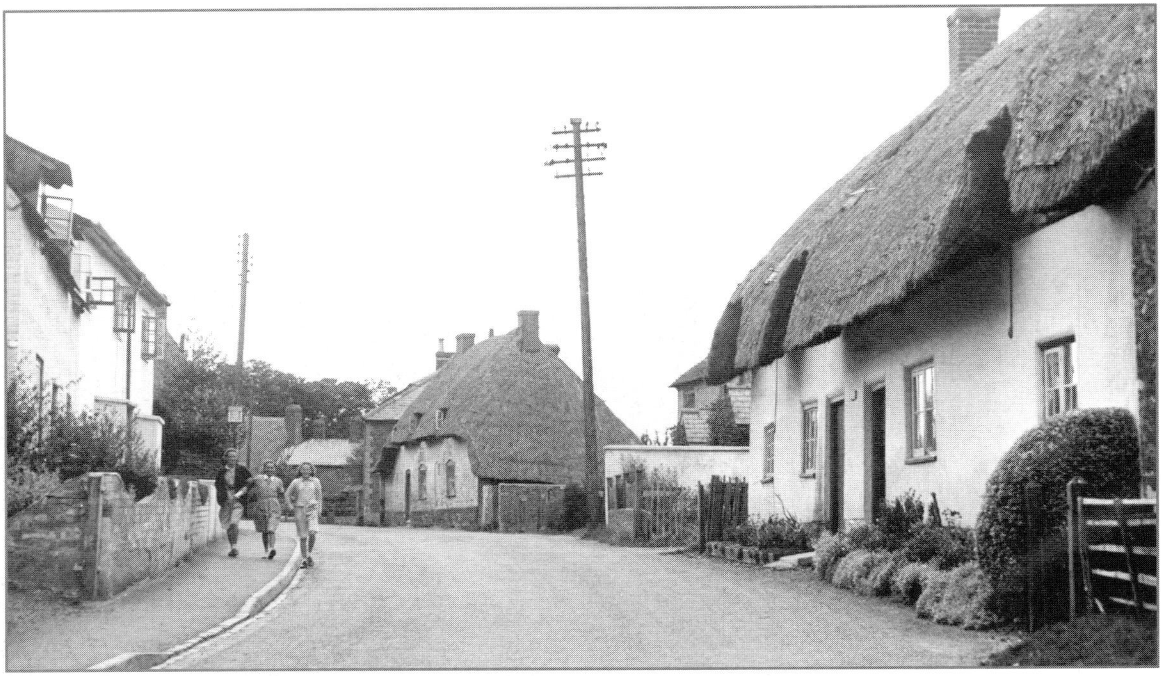

Upper Clatford, The Village c1955 U53011
Modern cleanliness - how different from the days when animals were driven or wandered through villages. Chalfont Cottage still had its thatch, but not for much longer after 1955.

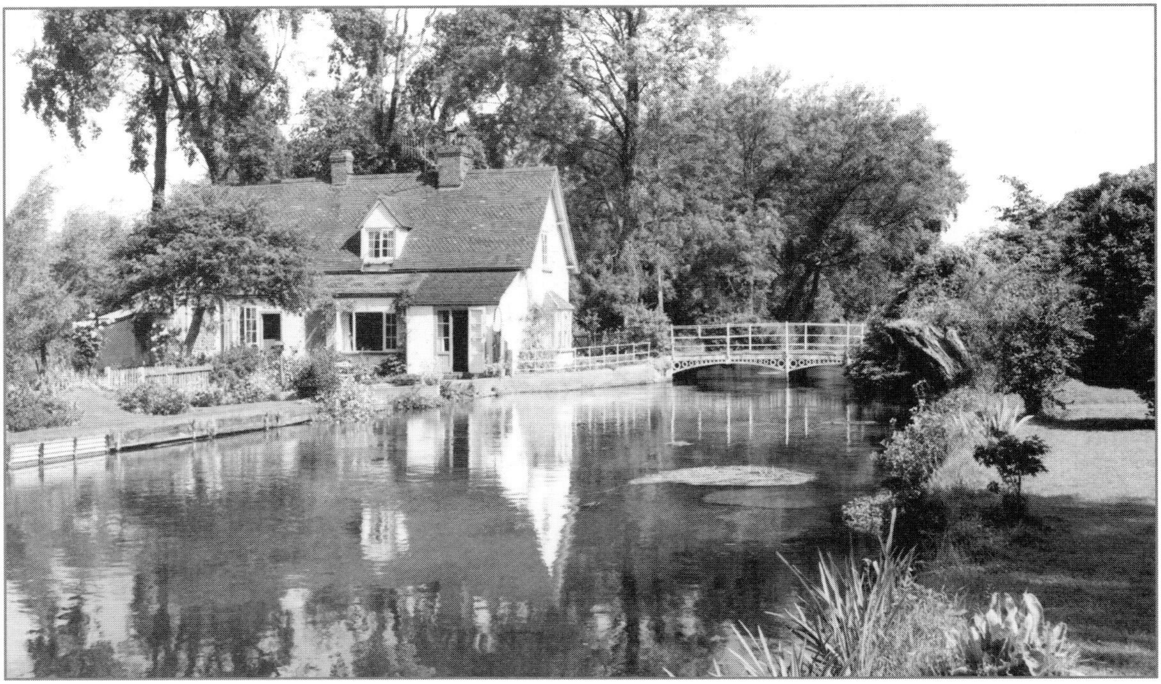

Upper Clatford, Fishing Cottage c1960 U53029
This cottage stands in an idyllic setting by the River Anton just outside the village. Tasker's bridge bears the date 1843.

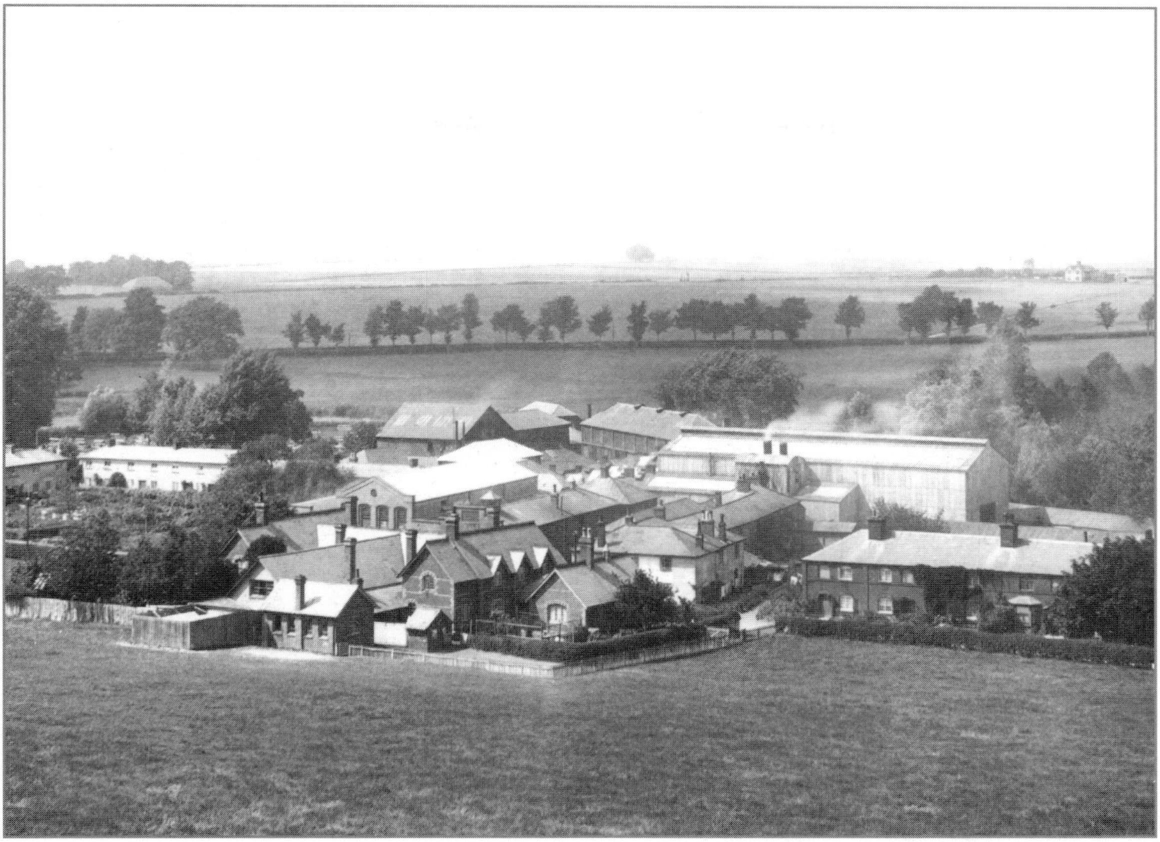

Anna Valley, Tasker's Ironworks 1899 43695
The Waterloo Iron Works opened in 1813 and closed in 1984, making way for housing. The schoolhouse survives complete with its arch into the works. At its peak in 1899, Tasker's made iron castings, columns and beams, and agricultural machines such as threshers, balers and steam traction engines. In World War II their Queen Mary Trailer was a famous transporter of aircraft. The 1867 Waterloo Workmen's Hall is now a private house.

Charlton, Hurstbourne Tarrant, Longparish and Harewood Forest

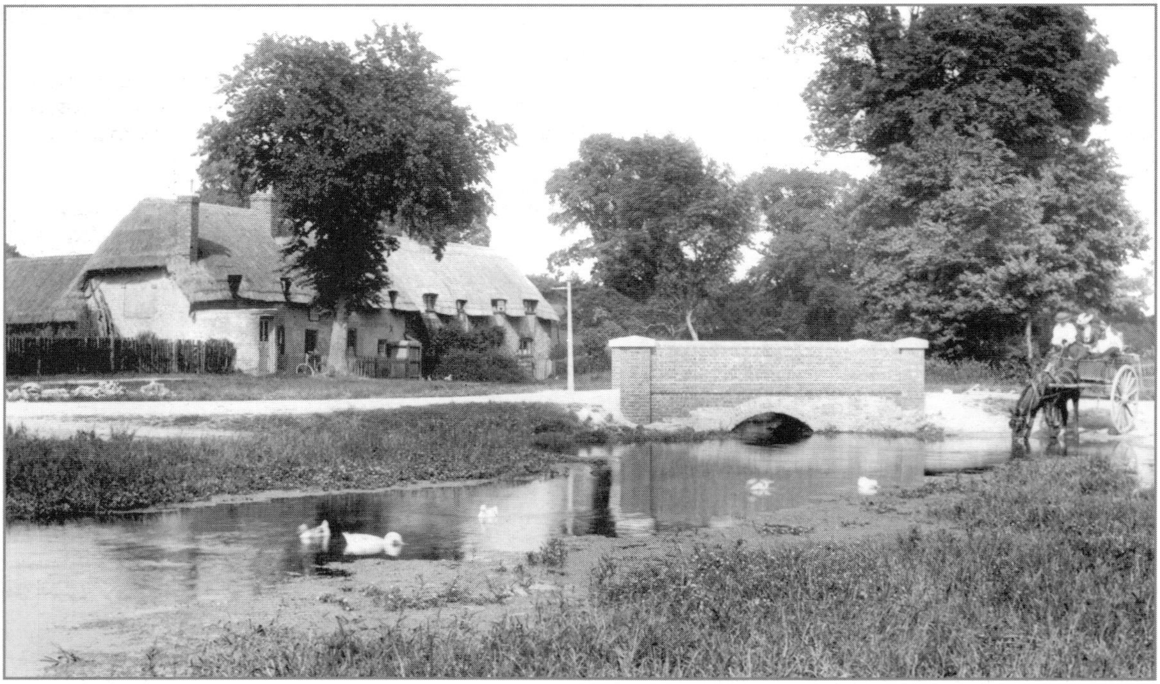

Charlton Village 1908 60101
In recent years, land to the west of the village has been developed for sports and recreation. To the north-east, houses have been built up to Charlton Nature Reserve. While the centre still retains its charm where the river passes through, the village is now almost continuous with Andover.

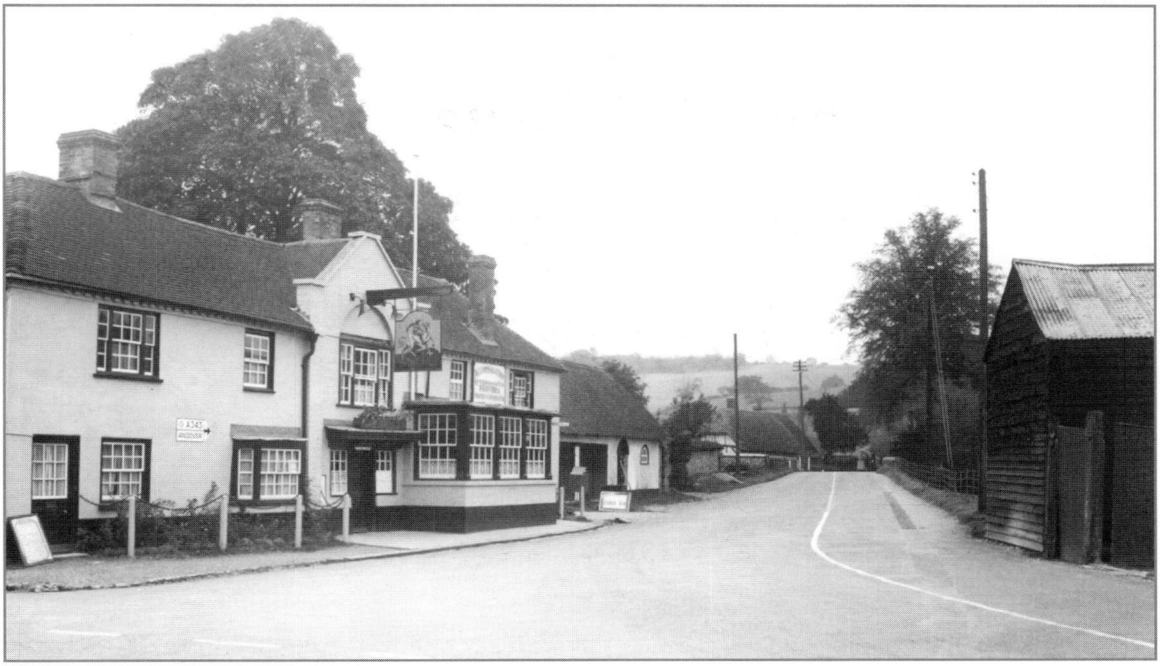

Hurstbourne Tarrant, The George and Dragon c1955 H417004

This comfortable pub, once an inn, lies under Hurstbourne Hill on what was the Andover turnpike to Newbury. It was near here that William Cobbett stayed with Joseph Blount at Rookery Farm. He said that the land at Uphusband (the former village name) was dry except when it rained. Flocks of sheep added beauty and in wet weather never injured the land, even when feeding off turnips.

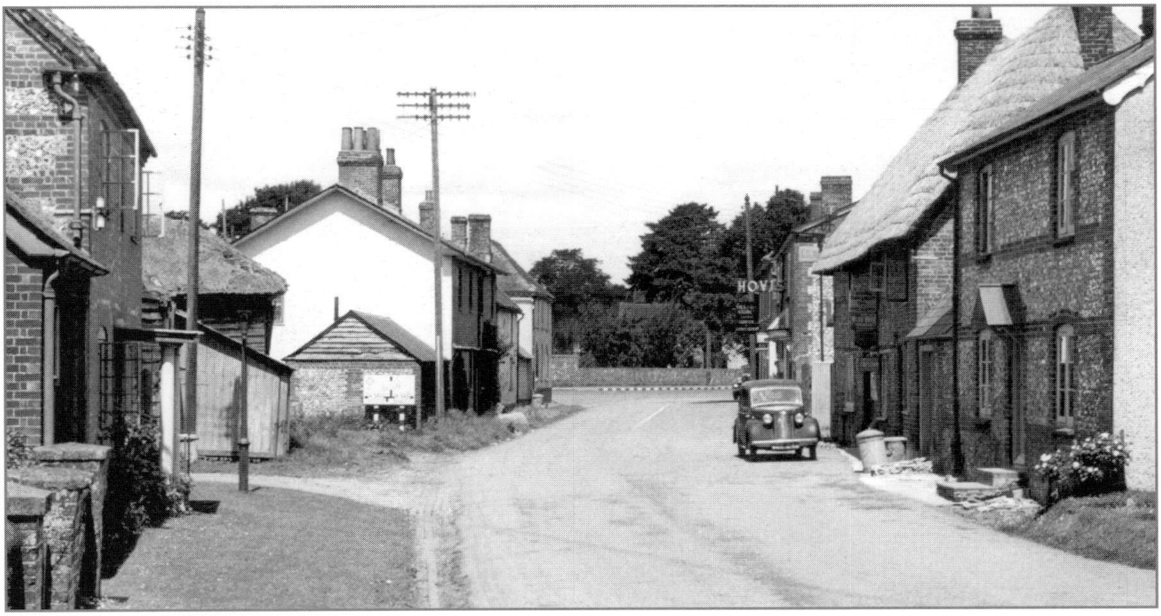

Hurstbourne Tarrant, The Village c1955 H417015

A neat Austin Ten is here heading for Newbury. Blount had a horse called Tinker which could be hired to help carts up Hurstbourne Hill. Having reached the top, Tinker would be released and could be relied upon to return to the farm every time.

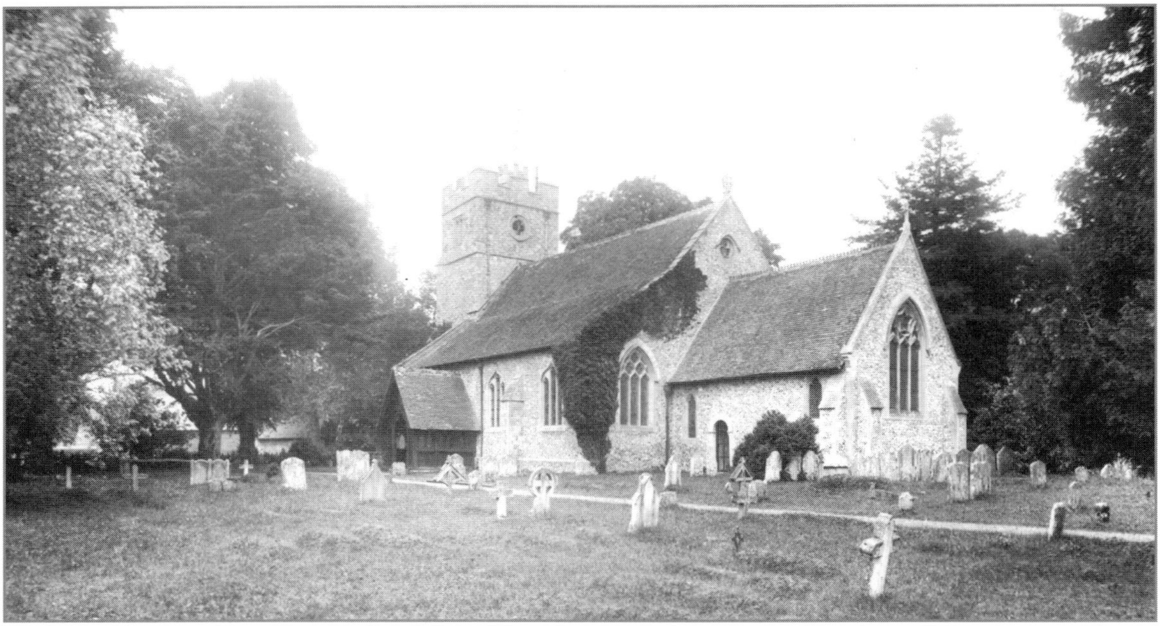

Longparish, St Nicholas' Church 1899 43700
This church is worth a visit and the east window by Morris and Co, as late as 1912, should not be missed. The nave and aisles date from about 1210 with a later square-topped tower. Henry Burnaby Greene, Rector, diverted the road around a pseudo-Saxon cross by the rectory gate. The lady living opposite retaliated by turning her house into an inn and calling it the Green Man.

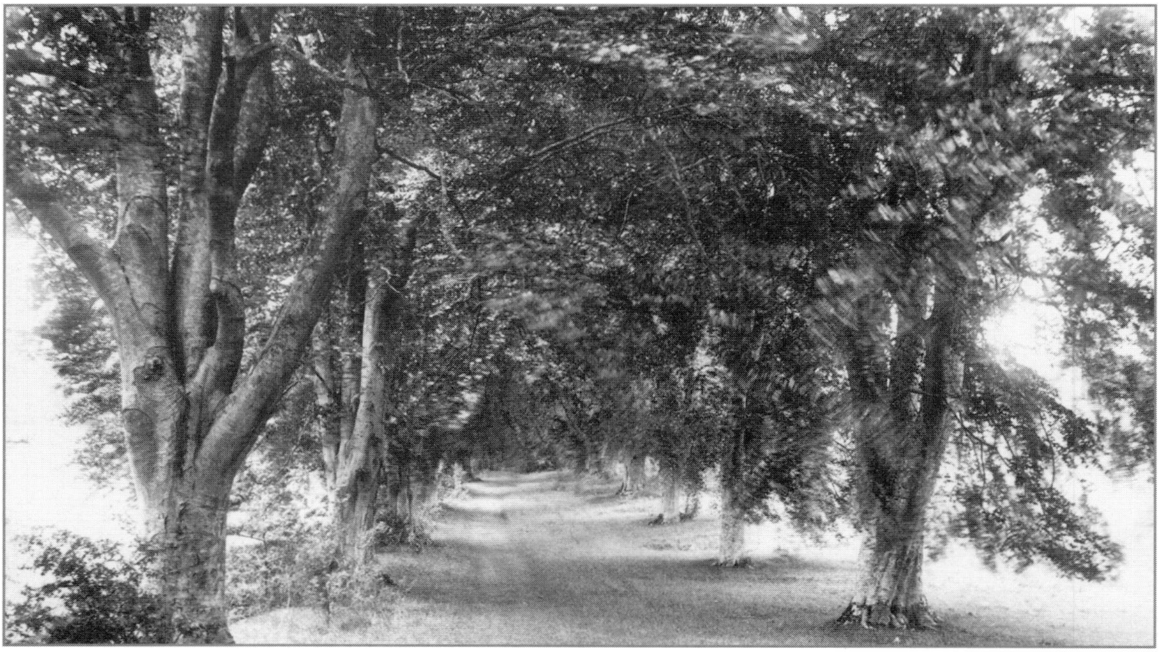

The Beech Avenue, Harewood Forest 1899 43702
During World War II the forest was laid with temporary roads and was used as a bomb dump and collection point for tanks and other equipment in preparation for the D-day invasion of Europe. Since the war it has returned to its original state with deer and foxes and a variety of other wildlife roaming the woods.

Index

Frith Book Co Titles

www.francisfrith.co.uk

The Frith Book Company publishes over 100 new titles each year. A selection of those currently available are listed below. For latest catalogue please contact Frith Book Co.

Town Books 96 pages, approx 100 photos. County and Themed Books 128 pages, approx 150 photos (unless specified). All titles hardback laminated case and jacket except those indicated pb (paperback)

Amersham, Chesham & Rickmansworth (pb)	1-85937-340-2	£9.99
Ancient Monuments & Stone Circles	1-85937-143-4	£17.99
Aylesbury (pb)	1-85937-227-9	£9.99
Bakewell	1-85937-113-2	£12.99
Barnstaple (pb)	1-85937-300-3	£9.99
Bath (pb)	1-85937419-0	£9.99
Bedford (pb)	1-85937-205-8	£9.99
Berkshire (pb)	1-85937-191-4	£9.99
Berkshire Churches	1-85937-170-1	£17.99
Blackpool (pb)	1-85937-382-8	£9.99
Bognor Regis (pb)	1-85937-431-x	£9.99
Bournemouth	1-85937-067-5	£12.99
Bradford (pb)	1-85937-204-x	£9.99
Brighton & Hove(pb)	1-85937-192-2	£8.99
Bristol (pb)	1-85937-264-3	£9.99
British Life A Century Ago (pb)	1-85937-213-9	£9.99
Buckinghamshire (pb)	1-85937-200-7	£9.99
Camberley (pb)	1-85937-222-8	£9.99
Cambridge (pb)	1-85937-422-0	£9.99
Cambridgeshire (pb)	1-85937-420-4	£9.99
Canals & Waterways (pb)	1-85937-291-0	£9.99
Canterbury Cathedral (pb)	1-85937-179-5	£9.99
Cardiff (pb)	1-85937-093-4	£9.99
Carmarthenshire	1-85937-216-3	£14.99
Chelmsford (pb)	1-85937-310-0	£9.99
Cheltenham (pb)	1-85937-095-0	£9.99
Cheshire (pb)	1-85937-271-6	£9.99
Chester	1-85937-090-x	£12.99
Chesterfield	1-85937-378-x	£9.99
Chichester (pb)	1-85937-228-7	£9.99
Colchester (pb)	1-85937-188-4	£8.99
Cornish Coast	1-85937-163-9	£14.99
Cornwall (pb)	1-85937-229-5	£9.99
Cornwall Living Memories	1-85937-248-1	£14.99
Cotswolds (pb)	1-85937-230-9	£9.99
Cotswolds Living Memories	1-85937-255-4	£14.99
County Durham	1-85937-123-x	£14.99
Croydon Living Memories	1-85937-162-0	£9.99
Cumbria	1-85937-101-9	£14.99
Dartmoor	1-85937-145-0	£14.99
Derby (pb)	1-85937-367-4	£9.99
Derbyshire (pb)	1-85937-196-5	£9.99
Devon (pb)	1-85937-297-x	£9.99
Dorset (pb)	1-85937-269-4	£9.99
Dorset Churches	1-85937-172-8	£17.99
Dorset Coast (pb)	1-85937-299-6	£9.99
Dorset Living Memories	1-85937-210-4	£14.99
Down the Severn	1-85937-118-3	£14.99
Down the Thames (pb)	1-85937-278-3	£9.99
Down the Trent	1-85937-311-9	£14.99
Dublin (pb)	1-85937-231-7	£9.99
East Anglia (pb)	1-85937-265-1	£9.99
East London	1-85937-080-2	£14.99
East Sussex	1-85937-130-2	£14.99
Eastbourne	1-85937-061-6	£12.99
Edinburgh (pb)	1-85937-193-0	£8.99
England in the 1880s	1-85937-331-3	£17.99
English Castles (pb)	1-85937-434-4	£9.99
English Country Houses	1-85937-161-2	£17.99
Essex (pb)	1-85937-270-8	£9.99
Exeter	1-85937-126-4	£12.99
Exmoor	1-85937-132-9	£14.99
Falmouth	1-85937-066-7	£12.99
Folkestone (pb)	1-85937-124-8	£9.99
Glasgow (pb)	1-85937-190-6	£9.99
Gloucestershire	1-85937-102-7	£14.99
Great Yarmouth (pb)	1-85937-426-3	£9.99
Greater Manchester (pb)	1-85937-266-x	£9.99
Guildford (pb)	1-85937-410-7	£9.99
Hampshire (pb)	1-85937-279-1	£9.99
Hampshire Churches (pb)	1-85937-207-4	£9.99
Harrogate	1-85937-423-9	£9.99
Hastings & Bexhill (pb)	1-85937-131-0	£9.99
Heart of Lancashire (pb)	1-85937-197-3	£9.99
Helston (pb)	1-85937-214-7	£9.99
Hereford (pb)	1-85937-175-2	£9.99
Herefordshire	1-85937-174-4	£14.99
Hertfordshire (pb)	1-85937-247-3	£9.99
Horsham (pb)	1-85937-432-8	£9.99
Humberside	1-85937-215-5	£14.99
Hythe, Romney Marsh & Ashford	1-85937-256-2	£9.99

Available from your local bookshop or from the publisher

Frith Book Co Titles (continued)

Ipswich (pb)	1-85937-424-7	£9.99
Ireland (pb)	1-85937-181-7	£9.99
Isle of Man (pb)	1-85937-268-6	£9.99
Isles of Scilly	1-85937-136-1	£14.99
Isle of Wight (pb)	1-85937-429-8	£9.99
Isle of Wight Living Memories	1-85937-304-6	£14.99
Kent (pb)	1-85937-189-2	£9.99
Kent Living Memories	1-85937-125-6	£14.99
Lake District (pb)	1-85937-275-9	£9.99
Lancaster, Morecambe & Heysham (pb)	1-85937-233-3	£9.99
Leeds (pb)	1-85937-202-3	£9.99
Leicester	1-85937-073-x	£12.99
Leicestershire (pb)	1-85937-185-x	£9.99
Lincolnshire (pb)	1-85937-433-6	£9.99
Liverpool & Merseyside (pb)	1-85937-234-1	£9.99
London (pb)	1-85937-183-3	£9.99
Ludlow (pb)	1-85937-176-0	£9.99
Luton (pb)	1-85937-235-x	£9.99
Maidstone	1-85937-056-x	£14.99
Manchester (pb)	1-85937-198-1	£9.99
Middlesex	1-85937-158-2	£14.99
New Forest	1-85937-128-0	£14.99
Newark (pb)	1-85937-366-6	£9.99
Newport, Wales (pb)	1-85937-258-9	£9.99
Newquay (pb)	1-85937-421-2	£9.99
Norfolk (pb)	1-85937-195-7	£9.99
Norfolk Living Memories	1-85937-217-1	£14.99
Northamptonshire	1-85937-150-7	£14.99
Northumberland Tyne & Wear (pb)	1-85937-281-3	£9.99
North Devon Coast	1-85937-146-9	£14.99
North Devon Living Memories	1-85937-261-9	£14.99
North London	1-85937-206-6	£14.99
North Wales (pb)	1-85937-298-8	£9.99
North Yorkshire (pb)	1-85937-236-8	£9.99
Norwich (pb)	1-85937-194-9	£8.99
Nottingham (pb)	1-85937-324-0	£9.99
Nottinghamshire (pb)	1-85937-187-6	£9.99
Oxford (pb)	1-85937-411-5	£9.99
Oxfordshire (pb)	1-85937-430-1	£9.99
Peak District (pb)	1-85937-280-5	£9.99
Penzance	1-85937-069-1	£12.99
Peterborough (pb)	1-85937-219-8	£9.99
Piers	1-85937-237-6	£17.99
Plymouth	1-85937-119-1	£12.99
Poole & Sandbanks (pb)	1-85937-251-1	£9.99
Preston (pb)	1-85937-212-0	£9.99
Reading (pb)	1-85937-238-4	£9.99
Romford (pb)	1-85937-319-4	£9.99
Salisbury (pb)	1-85937-239-2	£9.99
Scarborough (pb)	1-85937-379-8	£9.99
St Albans (pb)	1-85937-341-0	£9.99
St Ives (pb)	1-85937415-8	£9.99
Scotland (pb)	1-85937-182-5	£9.99
Scottish Castles (pb)	1-85937-323-2	£9.99
Sevenoaks & Tunbridge	1-85937-057-8	£12.99
Sheffield, South Yorks (pb)	1-85937-267-8	£9.99
Shrewsbury (pb)	1-85937-325-9	£9.99
Shropshire (pb)	1-85937-326-7	£9.99
Somerset	1-85937-153-1	£14.99
South Devon Coast	1-85937-107-8	£14.99
South Devon Living Memories	1-85937-168-x	£14.99
South Hams	1-85937-220-1	£14.99
Southampton (pb)	1-85937-427-1	£9.99
Southport (pb)	1-85937-425-5	£9.99
Staffordshire	1-85937-047-0	£12.99
Stratford upon Avon	1-85937-098-5	£12.99
Suffolk (pb)	1-85937-221-x	£9.99
Suffolk Coast	1-85937-259-7	£14.99
Surrey (pb)	1-85937-240-6	£9.99
Sussex (pb)	1-85937-184-1	£9.99
Swansea (pb)	1-85937-167-1	£9.99
Tees Valley & Cleveland	1-85937-211-2	£14.99
Thanet (pb)	1-85937-116-7	£9.99
Tiverton (pb)	1-85937-178-7	£9.99
Torbay	1-85937-063-2	£12.99
Truro	1-85937-147-7	£12.99
Victorian and Edwardian Cornwall	1-85937-252-x	£14.99
Victorian & Edwardian Devon	1-85937-253-8	£14.99
Victorian & Edwardian Kent	1-85937-149-3	£14.99
Vic & Ed Maritime Album	1-85937-144-2	£17.99
Victorian and Edwardian Sussex	1-85937-157-4	£14.99
Victorian & Edwardian Yorkshire	1-85937-154-x	£14.99
Victorian Seaside	1-85937-159-0	£17.99
Villages of Devon (pb)	1-85937-293-7	£9.99
Villages of Kent (pb)	1-85937-294-5	£9.99
Villages of Sussex (pb)	1-85937-295-3	£9.99
Warwickshire (pb)	1-85937-203-1	£9.99
Welsh Castles (pb)	1-85937-322-4	£9.99
West Midlands (pb)	1-85937-289-9	£9.99
West Sussex	1-85937-148-5	£14.99
West Yorkshire (pb)	1-85937-201-5	£9.99
Weymouth (pb)	1-85937-209-0	£9.99
Wiltshire (pb)	1-85937-277-5	£9.99
Wiltshire Churches (pb)	1-85937-171-x	£9.99
Wiltshire Living Memories	1-85937-245-7	£14.99
Winchester (pb)	1-85937-428-x	£9.99
Windmills & Watermills	1-85937-242-2	£17.99
Worcester (pb)	1-85937-165-5	£9.99
Worcestershire	1-85937-152-3	£14.99
York (pb)	1-85937-199-x	£9.99
Yorkshire (pb)	1-85937-186-8	£9.99
Yorkshire Living Memories	1-85937-166-3	£14.99

See Frith books on the internet www.francisfrith.co.uk

FRITH PRODUCTS & SERVICES

Francis Frith would doubtless be pleased to know that the pioneering publishing venture he started in 1860 still continues today. A hundred and forty years later, The Francis Frith Collection continues in the same innovative tradition and is now one of the foremost publishers of vintage photographs in the world. Some of the current activities include:

Interior Decoration

Today Frith's photographs can be seen framed and as giant wall murals in thousands of pubs, restaurants, hotels, banks, retail stores and other public buildings throughout the country. In every case they enhance the unique local atmosphere of the places they depict and provide reminders of gentler days in an increasingly busy and frenetic world.

Product Promotions

Frith products are used by many major companies to promote the sales of their own products or to reinforce their own history and heritage. Frith promotions have been used by Hovis bread, Courage beers, Scots Porage Oats, Colman's mustard, Cadbury's foods, Mellow Birds coffee, Dunhill pipe tobacco, Guinness, and Bulmer's Cider.

Genealogy and Family History

As the interest in family history and roots grows world-wide, more and more people are turning to Frith's photographs of Great Britain for images of the towns, villages and streets where their ancestors lived; and, of course, photographs of the churches and chapels where their ancestors were christened, married and buried are an essential part of every genealogy tree and family album.

Frith Products

All Frith photographs are available Framed or just as Mounted Prints and Posters (size 23 x 16 inches). These may be ordered from the address below. From time to time other products - Address Books, Calendars, Table Mats, etc - are available.

The Internet

Already twenty thousand Frith photographs can be viewed and purchased on the internet through the Frith websites and a myriad of partner sites.

For more detailed information on Frith companies and products, look at these sites:

www.francisfrith.co.uk
www.francisfrith.com
(for North American visitors)

See the complete list of Frith Books at:

www.francisfrith.co.uk

This web site is regularly updated with the latest list of publications from the Frith Book Company. If you wish to buy books relating to another part of the country that your local bookshop does not stock, you may purchase on-line.

For further information, trade, or author enquiries please contact us at the address below:

The Francis Frith Collection, Frith's Barn, Teffont, Salisbury, Wiltshire, England SP3 5QP.
Tel: +44 (0)1722 716 376 Fax: +44 (0)1722 716 881 Email: sales@francisfrith.co.uk

See Frith books on the internet www.francisfrith.co.uk

TO RECEIVE YOUR FREE MOUNTED PRINT

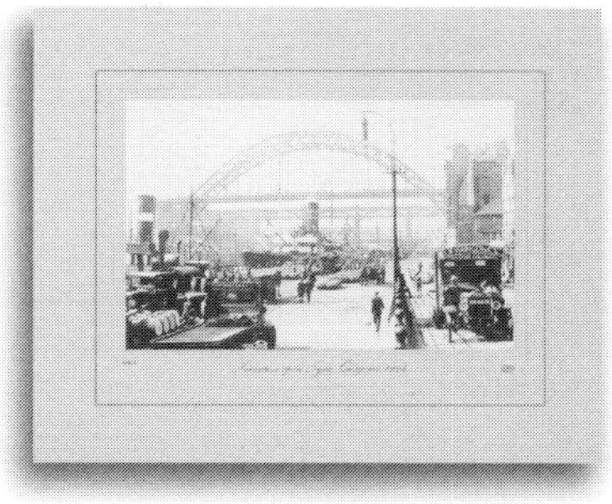

Mounted Print
Overall size 14 x 11 inches

Cut out this Voucher and return it with your remittance for £1.95 to cover postage and handling, to UK addresses. For overseas addresses please include £4.00 post and handling.
Choose any photograph included in this book. Your SEPIA print will be A4 in size, and mounted in a cream mount with burgundy rule line, overall size 14 x 11 inches.

Order additional Mounted Prints at HALF PRICE (only £7.49 each*)
If there are further pictures you would like to order, possibly as gifts for friends and family, purchase them at half price (no additional postage and handling required).

Have your Mounted Prints framed*
For an additional £14.95 per print you can have your chosen Mounted Print framed in an elegant polished wood and gilt moulding, overall size 16 x 13 inches (no additional postage and handling required).

*** IMPORTANT!**
These special prices are only available if ordered using the original voucher on this page (no copies permitted) and at the same time as your free Mounted Print, for delivery to the same address

Frith Collectors' Guild

From time to time we publish a magazine of news and stories about Frith photographs and further special offers of Frith products. If you would like 12 months FREE membership, please return this form.

Send completed forms to:
The Francis Frith Collection, Frith's Barn, Teffont, Salisbury, Wiltshire SP3 5QP

Voucher for FREE and Reduced Price Frith Prints

Picture no.	Page number	Qty	Mounted @ £7.49	Framed + £14.95	Total Cost
		1	**Free of charge***	£	£
			£7.49	£	£
			£7.49	£	£
			£7.49	£	£
			£7.49	£	£
			£7.49	£	£

Please allow 28 days for delivery *** Post & handling** £3.50

Book Title .... **Total Order Cost** £

Please do not photocopy this voucher. Only the original is valid, so please cut it out and return it to us.

I enclose a cheque / postal order for £ ....
made payable to 'The Francis Frith Collection'
OR please debit my Mastercard / Visa / Switch / Amex card
(credit cards please on all overseas orders)

Number ....
Issue No (Switch only) .... Valid from (Amex/Switch) ....
Expires .... Signature ....

Name Mr/Mrs/Ms ....
Address ....
....
....
.... Postcode ....
Daytime Tel No ....

VALID TO 31/12/08

The Francis Frith Collectors' Guild

Please enrol me as a member for 12 months free of charge.

Name Mr/Mrs/Ms ....
Address ....
....
....
.... Postcode ....

Free Print - see overleaf

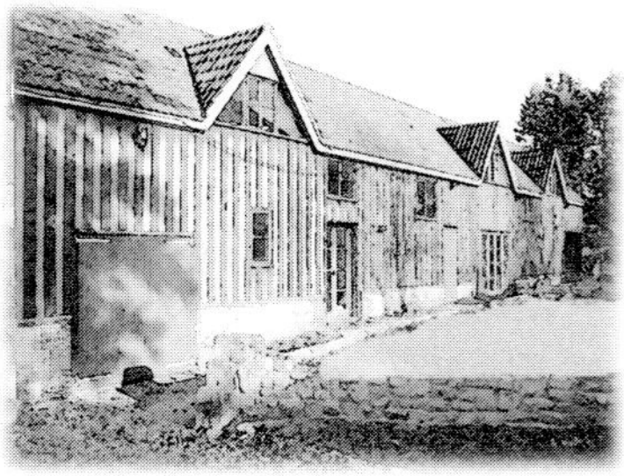

Would you like to find out more about Francis Frith?

We have recently recruited some entertaining speakers who are happy to visit local groups, clubs and societies to give an illustrated talk documenting Frith's travels and photographs. If you are a member of such a group and are interested in hosting a presentation, we would love to hear from you.

Our speakers bring with them a small selection of our local town and county books, together with sample prints. They are happy to take orders. A small proportion of the order value is donated to the group who have hosted the presentation. The talks are therefore an excellent way of fundraising for small groups and societies.

Can you help us with information about any of the Frith photographs in this book?

We are gradually compiling an historical record for each of the photographs in the Frith archive. It is always fascinating to find out the names of the people shown in the pictures, as well as insights into the shops, buildings and other features depicted.

If you recognize anyone in the photographs in this book, or if you have information not already included in the author's caption, do let us know. We would love to hear from you, and will try to publish it in future books or articles.

Our production team

Frith books are produced by a small dedicated team at offices in the converted Grade II listed 18th-century barn at Teffont near Salisbury, illustrated above. Most have worked with the Frith Collection for many years. All have in common one quality: they have a passion for the Frith Collection. The team is constantly expanding, but currently includes:

Jason Buck, John Buck, Douglas Burns, Heather Crisp, Isobel Hall, Rob Hames, Hazel Heaton, Peter Horne, James Kinnear, Tina Leary, Hannah Marsh, Eliza Sackett, Terence Sackett, Sandra Sanger, Shelley Tolcher, Susanna Walker, Clive Wathen and Jenny Wathen.